Stages of Meditation

Stages of Meditation

The Dalai Lama

root text by

Kamalashila

translated by

Venerable Geshe Lobsang Jordhen,
Losang Choephel Ganchenpa,
and Jeremy Russell

Snow Lion Publications
Ithaca, New York
Boulder, Colorado

Snow Lion Publications
P.O. Box 6483
Ithaca, New York 14851 USA
Tel: 607-273-8519
www.snowlionpub.com

This edition 2003

Printed in Canada on acid-free recycled paper

ISBN 1-55939-197-9

The Library of Congress catalogued the previous edition of this book as follows:

Bstan-'dzin-rgya-mtsho, Dalai Lama XIV, 1935-
Stages of meditation : [commentary] / the Dalai Lama ; root text by Kamalashila ; translated by Geshe Lobsang Jordhen, Losang Choephel Ganchenpa, and Jeremy Russell.
p. cm.
Includes biblographical references.
English, Sanskrit, Tibetan.
ISBN 1-55939-069-7 (alk. paper)
1. Kamalāśila, fl. 713-763 Bhāvanākrama. 2. Meditation, Buddhism. I. Geshe Lobsang Jordhen. II. Losang Choephel Ganchenpa. III. Russell, Jeremy. IV. Kamalasila, fl. 713-763. Bhavanakrama. Sanskrit and Tibetan. V. Title.

BQ3137.B88 2001
294.3'4435—dc21
00-044663

Contents

PREFACE

We are happy to be able to present here a translation of the intermediate *Stages of Meditation* by Kamalashila with a commentary by His Holiness the Dalai Lama. When His Holiness gave this commentary at Manali in 1989, we were inspired by a strong wish to make it available as a book. Since then we have worked on it when we could and are happy that it has now finally come to fruition.

Acharya Kamalashila was a great scholar-saint of the ninth century and a disciple of the great abbot Shantarakshita. It was due to the compassionate activities of such great teachers as these that a complete and unmistaken form of the Buddha's teaching flourished in Tibet. Kamalashila played a unique role in this because he was the first Indian scholar-saint to compose a significant text in Tibet with a view to the needs of the Tibetan people and with the intention of dispelling the misunderstandings then prevailing there. Unfortunately, due to the turmoil of our times, and particularly the tragedy that has befallen Tibet, serious students and practitioners have long been deprived of the opportunity of listening to, reading, thinking about, or meditating on such important texts. Realizing this, His Holiness the Dalai Lama has, despite the many pressing calls on his attention, made serious efforts to preserve this tradition, which fosters studying and putting into practice the meaning of important and rare texts such as this. Consequently he has taught *Stages of Meditation* on several occasions.

We are pleased to make available the commentary he gave in Manali, the small town at the head of the Kullu Valley in Himachal Pradesh that has longstanding links with Tibetans and the people of the Indo-Tibetan border region. It is our sincere wish that our humble efforts will contribute to the preservation of the unblemished teaching of Acharya Kamalashila. We hope that whatever positive imprints readers may derive from it may contribute to all sentient beings achieving the ultimate happiness of Buddhahood.

We dedicate whatever merit may be created through this work to the flourishing of the Buddhadharma, to peace among sentient beings, and to the long life of His Holiness the Dalai Lama and other great spiritual teachers and practitioners. We are grateful to Susan Kyser, our editor at Snow Lion, for her invaluable suggestions that have improved the final copy, and to everyone who has directly or indirectly contributed to bringing this project to fulfillment.

This book has been translated and edited by the following team: Geshe Lobsang Jordhen, a graduate of the Institute of Buddhist

Dialectics, Dharamsala, who since 1989 has been religious assistant and personal translator to His Holiness the Dalai Lama; Losang Choephel Ganchenpa, who also trained at the Institute of Buddhist Dialectics and has worked as a Buddhist translator for over a decade, first at the Library of Tibetan Works and Archives, Dharamsala, and later in Australia; and Jeremy Russell, who is editor of *Chö-Yang, the Voice of Tibetan Religion & Culture,* published by the Norbulingka Institute, Dharamsala.

Prologue

In the Indian language *Bhavanakrama,* and in the Tibetan language *Gompai Rimpa.*

Homage to the youthful Manjushri. I shall briefly explain the stages of meditation for those who follow the system of Mahayana sutras. The intelligent who wish to actualize omniscience extremely quickly should make deliberate effort to fulfill its causes and conditions.

The great spiritual master Kamalashila composed this text called the *Stages of Meditation* in three parts: the initial *Stages of Meditation*, the intermediate *Stages of Meditation,* and the last *Stages of Meditation.* Here I am explaining the intermediate *Stages of Meditation.* The essential subjects of this treatise are the awakening mind of bodhichitta and the perfect view. The spiritual paths that lead to the ultimate goal of Buddhahood are two: method and wisdom. These two qualities produce the physical body, or rupakaya, and the wisdom body, or dharmakaya, respectively. The first represents perfection of working for the welfare of other sentient beings and the second represents the perfection of one's own purposes. The methods for generating bodhichitta and the wisdom realizing emptiness together form the foundation of the Buddhist teachings, and this text provides a clear exposition of these two aspects of the Buddhist path to enlightenment.

When we take a closer look at these teachings, we come to understand that compassionate thought is the root of bodhichitta, or awakening mind. This thought of enlightenment must be put into practice in conjunction with the wisdom that realizes the ultimate nature of all phenomena, emptiness. This wisdom should be a union of special insight and a calmly abiding mind single-pointedly focused on its object, emptiness.

Most of you who are listening to this come from the Lahaul, Kinnaur, and Spiti regions of India, and most of you have a certain amount of education. However, the teaching technique I shall employ here is primarily oriented to those who don't believe in religion. In the process, I want to show how one can generate interest in religion in general and Buddhism in particular. There are many lines of reasoning that can help us develop interest in religion. In this way we may realize that religion is not based on mere faith, but that faith arises in conjunction with reason and logic. Basically there are two types of faith: that which is not based on any special reason and that which is backed by reason. In the case of the second type of faith, an individual examines the object of his or her belief and investigates its relevance to his or her needs and requirements. Faith is generated after seeing the reasons why it is advantageous. In Buddhism in general, and in the Mahayana path in particular, we examine the contents of the teachings and accept those that are logical and reasonable and reject those that are illogical. As such there are occasions when teachings that are in the Buddha's own words should not be taken literally, but need interpretation. Scriptural teachings that cannot stand logical analysis should not be taken literally, but require interpretation. On the other hand, scriptural teachings that can stand logical analysis should be taken literally. However, if we search for another scriptural authority to distinguish those scriptures that are to be understood literally and those that are to be interpreted, we will fall into the fallacy of infinite regress. We must examine both types of scriptural teachings with logic. Therefore, we can see that in the study of Buddhist scriptures, logical analysis has a very important place.

Before you embark on your investigation, it is essential that you study the techniques for testing the object of your analysis. For people who want to follow the Buddha's teachings in practice, mere faith is not enough. Faith should be backed by reason. When you study, follow a logical method. While I am teaching, I want you to pay good attention; make notes or use other means to be able to retain what I teach.

Let me begin by explaining what we mean by blessing when we talk about a lama's blessing or the blessing of the Dharma in the Buddhist context. Blessing must arise from within your own mind. It is not something that comes from outside, even though we talk about a lama's blessing or the blessing of the Three Objects of Refuge. When the positive qualities of your mind increase and negativities decrease, that is what blessing means. The Tibetan word for blessing [*byin rlab,* pronounced "chin-lap"] can be broken into two parts—*byin* means "magnificent potential," and *rlab* means "to transform." So *byin rlab* means transforming into magnificent potential. Therefore, blessing refers to the development of virtuous qualities that you did not previously have and the improvement of those good qualities that you have already developed. It also means decreasing the defilements of the mind that obstruct the generation of wholesome qualities. So actual blessing is received when the mind's virtuous attributes gain strength and its defective characteristics weaken or deteriorate.

The text says, "The intelligent who wish to actualize omniscience extremely quickly should make deliberate effort to fulfill its causes and conditions." What this means is that this book primarily deals with the procedures and practice of meditation, rather than an elaborate analysis of the objects that are refuted or presented in a more philosophical work. It is not that there are two separate and unrelated sets of Buddhist treatises—that some treatises are only the subject of discourse and others are only manuals of practice. All scriptures contain teachings to help tame and control the mind. Nevertheless, there can definitely be different levels of emphasis. Certain practices and texts are primarily suited to study and contemplation, and there are other texts that are taught with special emphasis on meditational procedures. This text is one of the latter. Therefore, in accordance with its content, it is called *Stages of Meditation.* And, as the title suggests, the text describes how a spiritual path can be developed in the mindstream of a meditator in a proper sequence, and not in a scattered piece-meal fashion.

Among the three parts of the *Stages of Meditation*, this is the middle part. Acharya Kamalashila initially taught it in his own Indian language. The text begins with its Sanskrit title, mention of which is intended to benefit the reader by creating an aptitude for this sacred language in her or his mind. Citing the title in the literary language of India has a historical dimension as well. Since the dawn of civilization in the Snowy Land of Tibet, and with the gradual development of the Tibetan nation, there has been a natural association with neighboring countries. In retrospect it appears that Tibetans have adopted many good socio-cultural elements from their neighbors. For instance, India, our neighbor to the south, was the source of religion and cultural systems and subjects that enrich the mind. Similarly, other ancient cultures and sciences like medicine, Buddhist philosophy, Sanskrit, etc., were introduced from India, home of many great scholars. Thus we Tibetans have a tradition of revering India as the Holy Land. China was known for its good food and its great variety of vegetables. In the Tibetan language we use the same word for vegetable as in Chinese, and even today we continue to use Chinese words for many vegetables. This is what we imported from China. Similarly, because Mongolian garments are well suited to a cold climate, Tibetans have copied some of their styles. So, over the centuries that Tibetans have been in contact with their neighbors, we have imported many good things and developed our own distinctive socio-cultural characteristics. When the text begins with the phrase, "In the Indian language," it indicates the authenticity of the text—that it originated in the treatises of Indian masters.

Then the text says, "In the Tibetan language," and the Tibetan title is provided. This indicates that the text was translated into the language of another country, Tibet. The Tibetan language is rich enough to accurately express great treatises, including the sutras and their commentaries. Over the centuries the Tibetan language has been a major medium both for the discourse and the practice aspects of Buddhism. Even today, it appears that Tibetan is almost the only language in the world that can fully communicate the entire Buddhist teachings contained in the Hinayana, Mahayana, and Tantric canons. Tibetan is therefore a very important language and it is especially valuable in relation to Buddhism.

"Homage to the youthful Manjushri." This is the verse of obeisance and supplication by the translator. The translators start their work by paying homage so that they will be able to complete their work without facing any obstacles. It also represents their aspiration to fulfill their temporary and ultimate purposes. Supplication is made to Manjushri following a decree promulgated by the religious kings in the past. The intention was to clearly indicate to which of the three divisions [the *pitakas*, or baskets] of the Buddha's teachings any sutra or commentary belongs. Supplication is made to all Buddhas and Bodhisattvas if a text belongs to the Collection of Discourses. And if a text belongs to the Collection of Knowledge, supplication is made to Manjushri. In order to indicate that a certain text belongs to the Collection of Discipline, supplication is made to the Omniscient

Ones. So the supplication by the translator conforms to traditional practice. The main thesis of this treatise concerns establishing selflessness by relying on that single-pointed concentration which is a union of special insight and a calmly abiding mind. And as it belongs to the Collection of Knowledge, supplication is made to Manjushri.

With the phrase, "for those who follow the system of Mahayana sutras," the author briefly reveals the process of meditation for those who study this treatise. Now the question arises: What is the ultimate goal of those who practice the Mahayana teachings? And the answer is Buddhahood. What does Buddhahood mean? One who possesses a transcendental all-knowing wisdom is a Buddha, and this state is referred to as Buddhahood. Since the final goal of the Mahayana teachings is to attain this omniscient state, the practitioner needs to investigate closely the means and methods that lead to this realization. Through such investigation, he or she must strive to pursue the correct and complete course for realizing the omniscient state. This is a brief summary of the theme of this book.

Introduction

In the words of the Superior Nagarjuna,

> If you wish to attain the unsurpassed enlightenment
> For yourself and the world,
> The root is generation of an altruistic thought
> That is stable and firm like a mountain,
> An all-embracing compassion,
> And a transcendent wisdom free of duality.

Those of us who desire happiness for others and ourselves temporarily and in the long term should be motivated to attain the omniscient state. Compassion, altruistic thought, and the perfect view are the fundamentals and lifeblood of the path to highest enlightenment. At this juncture, we have faith in the doctrine of Lord Buddha and have access to his teachings. We are free from the major obstacles and have met the contributory factors such that we can study the vast and profound aspects of Buddha's teaching, contemplate their contents, and meditate on their meaning. We must therefore use all these opportunities so that we won't have cause for regret in the future and so that we don't prove unkind to ourselves. What Kadam Geshe Sangpuwa has said strikes at the central theme. This verse greatly moves me from the very heart:

> Teaching and listening are proper when they are beneficial to the mind. Controlled and disciplined behavior is the sign of having heard teachings. Afflictions are reduced as a sign of meditation. A yogi is the one who understands reality.

One thing that should be very clear is that Dharma teachings have only one purpose: to discipline the mind. Teachers should pay attention and see to it that their teachings benefit the minds of their students. Their instructions must be based upon their personal experience of understanding the Dharma. Students, too, should attend teachings with a desire to benefit their minds. They must make an all-out effort to control their undisciplined minds. I might therefore urge that we should be diligent in following the instructions of the great Kadampa Geshes. They have advised that there should be integration of the mind and Dharma. On the other hand, if knowledge and practice are treated as unrelated and distinct entities, then the training can prove ineffective. In the process of our spiritual practice, we must examine ourselves thoroughly and use Dharma as a mirror in which to see reflected the defects of our body, speech, and mind. Both the teacher and student must be motivated to benefit themselves and others through the practice of the teachings. As we find in the *lam rim* prayers:

Motivated by powerful compassion,
May I be able to expound the treasure of Buddhadharma,
Conveying it to new places
And places where it has degenerated.

The Buddha's doctrine is not something physical. Therefore, the restoration and spread of Buddhism depends on our inner spirit, or the continuum of our mind. When we are able to reduce the defects of the mind, its good qualities increase. Thus, effecting positive transformations is what the preservation and promotion of the Buddha's doctrine means. It is obvious that the doctrine is not a tangible entity, that it cannot be sold or bought in the marketplace or physically constructed. We should pay attention to the fundamentals, like the practice of the three trainings—renunciation, the awakening mind of bodhichitta, and the wisdom realizing emptiness.

The responsibility for the preservation and furthering of Buddhist doctrine lies upon those of us who have faith in that doctrine; this in turn depends on our attraction to the Buddha and respect for him. If we don't do anything constructive and expect that others will, then obviously nothing is possible. The first step is to cultivate within our minds those positive qualities taught by the Buddha. After properly disciplining our own minds, then we may hope to help discipline others' minds. The great Tsongkhapa has clearly stated that those who have not disciplined themselves have hardly any chance of disciplining others. Acharya Dharmakirti has taught this principle in very lucid terms:

When the technique is obscure [to you],
Explanation is naturally difficult.

Bodhisattvas with such an intention ultimately aim to attain the state of enlightenment. For this purpose, they engage in the practices of eliminating the disturbing emotions that afflict the mind. At the same time they endeavor to cultivate spiritual insights. It is by following such a process of eliminating negative qualities and cultivating positive ones that Bodhisattvas become capable of helping other sentient beings. The *Commentary on (Dignaga's) "Compendium of Valid Cognition"* also says:

> The compassionate ones employ all means
> To alleviate the miseries of beings.

Therefore, those of us who believe in the Buddha's teachings should try our best to generate virtues. This is extremely important. It is especially relevant in this age when the Buddha's doctrine is degenerating. We Tibetans are making noise and criticizing the Chinese for the destruction they have caused in our country. But the important thing is that as followers of Buddhism we must diligently adhere to its principles. The teachings are only purposeful when we see the advantages of practicing, undertake the discipline, and effect positive transformations in our hearts. Listening to lectures on other subjects has a different purpose—there we aim to gain ideas and information.

You might wonder what are the signs of a true Dharma practitioner. Practice should begin with the ethical discipline of abstaining from the ten non-virtuous actions. Every negativity of body, speech, and mind should be properly identified and its antidotes fully understood. With this basic knowledge, an individual should eliminate negative actions like stealing, lying, and so forth, and practice honesty, kindness, and other virtuous deeds. Ordained monks and nuns have to follow the rules of monastic discipline. These are meant to discipline the way one wears the monastic robes, communicates with others, and so forth. Even the manner of looking at other people and the correct ways of addressing other people are taught in the rules of monastic discipline.

For a Dharma practitioner, one of the major challenges is to counter our disturbing emotions and finally free ourselves from them. The difficulty of this is due to the simple truth that disturbing emotions have from beginningless time caused us to suffer all kinds of miseries. If someone bullies us or an enemy persecutes us, then we raise a hue and cry. External enemies, however brutal they are, only affect us during one lifetime. They have no power to harm us beyond this life. On the other hand, disturbing emotions are our inner enemies and can definitely cause disaster in future lives. These are, in fact, our worst enemies.

The real test for a Dharma practitioner comes from this angle: if our disturbing emotions are reduced, then our practice has been effective. This is the main criterion in determining a true practitioner, regardless of how holy we appear externally. The whole purpose of meditation is to lessen the deluded afflictions of our mind and eventually eradicate them from their very roots. By learning and practicing the profound and vast aspects of the teaching, a practitioner with prolonged familiarity with and meditation on selflessness eventually gains an understanding of reality.

We are engaged in teaching and listening, and it is essential to know the proper ways, the effective methods, of listening to the teaching. This constitutes the elimination of the three defects of a listener (likened to a vessel), and the cultivation of the six favorable intentions. The first of the three defects is listening in a way that is like an upside down container. This means that physically we may be attending to the teachings but mentally we are busy somewhere else. So when someone is teaching, we are in fact not listening at all. In such a case we have no interest in the teachings and in fact do not hear anything that is taught. This is obviously a great obstacle to learning, and we must eliminate this problem and attend to the teaching with keen interest.

The second of the defects is to listen in a way that is like a container with holes. This means that even though we are listening to the teachings, we do not retain their contents. In this case we lack mindfulness and memory. Practice of Dharma means that we should be able to benefit from what we have heard. It is not a pastime, like listening to a story. The teachings give us guidance on how to live meaningful lives and how to develop proper attitudes. So in order to benefit from the teachings, we must retain them with mindfulness. In all kinds of learning processes, listening, reading, etc., we must pay full attention and should endeavor to remember their contents. When our interest is halfhearted, we only remember half the points, and we retain them for only a short time. We should reflect and think about whatever we have heard, over and over again. In this way, the knowledge will stay in our mind for a long time. Another technique for remembering instructions is debate as it is practiced in the traditional debating schools.

The third defect of a listener concerns the motivation, and is likened to a vessel containing poison. When we listen to the teachings, we must avoid deluded motives. All activities, particularly Dharma practices such as listening to and reading scriptural texts, must be done with a wholesome motivation. We should aim to control the undisciplined mind, and then gradually attain the state of Buddhahood to benefit all sentient beings. I urge you not to treat Dharma knowledge like any other kind of science just to earn a living.

Now let me turn to the main topic, the text by Kamalashila known as the *Stages of Meditation*. The author was immensely kind to Tibet. The great Tsongkhapa referred to him as an honorable scholar and the title is befitting. Of the several treatises he wrote, *Illumination of the Middle Way* and this text are the most highly respected.

The transmission lineage of the three *Stages of Meditation* texts is fairly rare. In the central and southwestern regions of Tibet, its transmission was not widely known. Maybe it was available in isolated and remote areas. Khunnu Lama Tenzin Gyaltsen received the lineage in Kham, and Serkong Rinpoche received it from him. At that time, I was not able to receive the transmission, although I wanted to. I thought that since the text is not very long there wouldn't be much difficulty in receiving it later. Instead, I put my efforts into receiving teachings on some of the major treatises like the *Great Commentary on Kalachakra* by Buton Rinchen Drup, the *Summary Tantra on Kalachakra*, and the six volumes of the *Annotations of the Great Commentary Called Stainless Light*.

I was away in Switzerland when I received a telegram saying that Serkong Rinpoche had passed away and Yongzin Ling

Rinpoche was in poor health. Then it struck me that I was paying the price for my laziness in not having taken teachings on the *Stages of Meditation* texts. My mind was filled with sorrow and a sense of loss. Afterwards, I would ask who held its lineage of transmission whenever I met lamas and geshes. Once, when I was in Bodhgaya, I met the Sakya abbot Sangye Tenzin. He told me that he had received teachings on the *Stages of Meditation* from an old lama from Kham who was in Lhasa on pilgrimage. Later, I thought that since Khunnu Lama Rinpoche had also received the teaching from Kham, the lineage would be the same. I also thought that it would be fine to receive the teaching.

Previously when I embarked on new texts, I would consult Yongzin Ling Rinpoche. By then he had passed away. At that time, Ven. Gen Nyima was also at Bodhgaya. So I told him the situation and asked for his opinion. He said that it was a good idea. In this way I received the teaching transmission from the Sakya abbot Sangye Tenzin. I felt very happy and fortunate, and that automatically freed me from feelings of remorse. This Sakya abbot is quite well-known and used to be a respected master in Sakya itself. Now he is in his eighties. It seems there are no written commentaries on this text; at least I haven't seen any. The great Tsongkhapa quotes from it at length in his *Great Stages of the Path,* so I think it would be appropriate if I supplement my commentary from there.

Kamalashila did a wonderful service for the Buddha's doctrine. With a steadfast and kind motivation, he established a perfect foundation for the Buddha's teaching during his time in Tibet. The Tibetan religious king Trisong Detsen invited Acharya

Shantarakshita and Guru Rinpoche Padmasambhava. These three great beings were extremely kind to the Snowy Land of Tibet. It was through their collaboration that a complete form of Buddhism, including the tantras, was properly established in Tibet. Acharya Shantarakshita saw the possibility of misunderstanding and misinterpreting the philosophy, and so he left instructions to invite Kamalashila when such occasions arose. History reveals that these were the reasons Kamalashila was invited to Tibet and composed the *Stages of Meditation.* At the end of the first part, the author states that he composed the text at the request of King Trisong Detsen.

For the benefit of the Tibetan people and to establish the Buddha's doctrine among them, the great Kamalashila very kindly came to Tibet. The three parts of the *Stages of Meditation* were written in Tibet and the Chinese Hvashang became the catalyst for the composition. The content of his general philosophy is a different matter, but the Chinese Hvashang's interpretation of the Buddhist view was definitely mistaken. Acharya Kamalashila wrote this text to preempt the advancement of those wrong views. What we may note here is that the great beings in those days exhibited much scholastic and moral strength. They used very refined language while refuting wrong views and didn't target their opponents as individuals. What they actually did was to formulate a lucid and clear presentation of the fundamental philosophical view, meditation, and conduct as taught by the Buddha. In that fashion, the Buddha's doctrine outshone the inferior and wrong views, which declined on their own. So this precious text has a special karmic link with Tibet, the Land of Snows.

It is obvious that the author Kamalashila was immeasurably kind to the Tibetans. But history reveals that the Tibetans made some mistakes instead of showing proper gratitude. Certain inappropriate incidents occurred. Looking at it from another angle, it was something like the saying in Tibetan, "Where the Dharma flourishes, the devil is also active." In order for well-founded temporal and spiritual institutions to last in Tibet, Guru Rinpoche created favorable conditions and blessed the environment. Even during such a time, there were people saying unhelpful things. It seems, at times, even the king did not fulfill all the wishes of Guru Rinpoche.

It is sad to note these things. Of course, there are other ways of looking at it. Buddhas and Bodhisattvas have nothing to do save work in the interest of all sentient beings. Lord Avalokiteshvara has a special link with Tibet and has done great kind deeds through numerous manifestations. We Tibetans, however, face unending problems even up to the present time. Still we must not lose heart. The international situation is fluid and constantly changing. There is support for the truth, and truth is precious. We have so far been able to establish proper foundations for our future. We should all work diligently to fulfill our individual interests of this life and the lives beyond, paying equal attention to the common cause. We are all fortunate to be able to study this wonderful text. It would be wise on our part to learn its guiding principles and try to transform our lives.

Within the context of Buddhist teachings, the generation of a positive attitude is very important. I urge you to listen with a wholesome motivation, thinking "I shall listen to the intermediate *Stages of Meditation* by the great Kamalashila in order to attain supreme Buddhahood for the sake of sentient beings vast as the expanse of space." The quality of any action of body, speech, and mind is primarily determined by the motivation. Thus any action done with positive motivation brings virtue and happiness and becomes a cause to attain Buddhahood in the long run. On the other hand, if a good or healthy motivation is missing, then even apparently spiritual practices could bring negative consequences in place of virtue. Since the line between them can be very thin at times, individuals need to pay extra attention to this aspect.

In this text the author presents the essence of the path of both the Hinayana and the Mahayana vehicles. He expounds the mode of practicing conventional bodhichitta and the six perfections with special emphasis on calm abiding meditation and special insight. Those of you who are new to Buddhism and not familiar with the modes and procedures of practicing the teachings should try to form a coherent understanding of this text, because on the basis of this knowledge you will be able to understand other treatises without great difficulty. This text can be like a key that opens the door to all other major Buddhist scriptures.

Chapter 1

What Is the Mind?

It is not possible for omniscience to be produced without causes, because if it were everything could always be omniscient. If things were produced without reliance on something else, they could exist without constraint—there would be no reason why everything could not be omniscient. Therefore, since all functional things arise only occasionally, they depend strictly on their causes. Omniscience too is rare because it does not occur at all times and in all places, and everything cannot become omniscient. Therefore, it definitely depends on causes and conditions.

According to this text, there are two types of existent phenomena: those that exist permanently and those that exist at some times but not at others. What is the implication of this second kind—existing at times but not existing at others? Such a question naturally arises. The implication is that temporary things depend on causes. The fact that certain things are produced at certain times proves the existence of causes. To say that certain things are produced at some times but not at others indicates that they are not independently produced, but rather that they depend on other conditions. Therefore, all those phenomena that are produced at some times but not others depend on causes and conditions, and they are of various types. Causes are of different types, such as substantial cause, direct cause, indirect cause, cause of equal state, concomitant cause, and so forth. Similarly, there are various types of conditions, like objective condition, causal condition, immediate condition, and so forth. So those phenomena that depend on causes and conditions change by nature; they do not abide in one place and they are not permanent.

Conditioned phenomena in turn can be classed under three categories—form, consciousness, and neither of the two. Form consists of such aspects as shape, color, and so forth, which can be seen by the eyes and touched by the hands. Consciousness has neither shape nor color and cannot be measured in any physical terms, but it exists in its nature and ability to feel and sense. Time, on the other hand, has neither form nor consciousness and belongs to the third category.

Omniscient transcendental wisdom refers to the consciousness that knows everything. Omniscience is not a quality found in soil, stones, rocks, or mountains. It is produced by something whose function is awareness of objects, and therefore it cannot be produced by anything that lacks the property of awareness. Of course, the state of omniscience is the ultimate goal encompassing every perfection, and of the three categories of conditioned phenomena it belongs to the category of consciousness.

Knowing or understanding is the function of consciousness. For example, when we say, "I understand" or "I see," and we have an experience or feeling about something, the experience is activated by consciousness. When the eye consciousness sees a physical form, we say, "I see the physical form," and when the mind consciousness experiences happiness or pain, we say, "I am happy," or "I am in pain." Thus, when we say, "I experience," "I see," or "I hear," and so forth, it is consciousness that acts as the agent. That which possesses the function of knowing is consciousness.

Consciousnesses vary in the scope of their knowledge and in their intensity or sharpness. An obvious example is the consciousness of a human being, compared to an animal's consciousness. The human being's perception is much broader and it understands a much greater variety of objects. The consciousnesses of human beings vary with education and experience—the more educated you are and the more experience you have, the broader your consciousness. Knowledge and understanding develop on the basis of a consciousness that has the ability to perceive its objects. When the necessary conditions are met, its ability to perceive increases, the scope of its objects of knowledge expands, and understanding deepens. In this way the mind can develop its full potential.

Omniscience is the full consummation, or perfection, of the mind's ability to perceive objects. It is omniscient in the sense that it can know each and every thing without being obstructed by differences of time and space. All-knowing wisdom arises from consciousness and by definition it is produced by causes and conditions. This implies that even omniscient wisdom cannot come about without its causes. If this were not the case, and an omniscient mind could arise without causes, it would imply that every consciousness was omniscient. This is because if things are produced without causes and conditions, either they must exist at all times or they must be completely non-existent. "If things were produced without reliance on other things, they would not be liable to be obstructed at any place." This is to say that if things were produced without depending on other causes and conditions, there is no logical reason why they should be obstructed at any point. Since this is not the case, it is logical that everything cannot be transformed into omniscience. For these reasons, functional phenomena can be produced at certain times and are not produced at other times. At a certain point in time, when favorable conditions come about and adverse conditions are absent, a consciousness can be transformed into omniscience that has the knowledge of all phenomena.

Since things are not produced at all times and in all places, the implication is that they depend on causes and conditions. Within the framework of dependence on causes and conditions, those who aspire to the final fruit of omniscience should generate the causes and conditions—the complete and correct causes and conditions. Besides this, aspirants must be highly motivated in their pursuit. Therefore, it is taught that omniscience depends on causes and conditions.

As explained in Asanga's *Compendium of Knowledge* with reference to effects being generated by their causes and conditions, the conditions are the unwavering condition, the impermanent condition, and the potential condition. What has been said earlier concerns the impermanent condition. When we ask how omniscience can be generated out of consciousness, we are talking about its potential condition. The ability to be aware of objects is an innate quality of consciousness. The very nature of consciousness is that it is clear and aware. It arises in the aspect of the object it apprehends. This attribute of awareness is not something newly created by other factors.

Now the question is how that awareness can grow and expand to a limitless scope. The ability to be aware of its objects is innate to consciousness, but there are things that impede the mind from opening up to the state of complete knowledge. The next question is how those obstacles come about. We need to consider how such obstacles can be removed. What obstructs consciousness from being aware of its object is the ignorance that is a misconception of true existence, also referred to as the ignorance holding to one extreme, the extreme of reification.

When we speak of ignorance, what we mean is that the consciousness either lacks some favorable condition, or some adverse condition is obstructing it from being aware of its object. Of the many types of ignorance, ignorance that is a misconception of true existence is the root, the power holder, so to speak. And this ignorance is the chief obstacle. We need to come to the conclusion through analysis that this ignorance is something that can be removed and eliminated. The defects of the mind arise primarily due to ignorance and its latent potential. We need to investigate and determine whether ignorance can be separated from the mind, and whether ignorance can come to an end. Ignorance in this context is not mere stupidity, but the ignorance that is a misconception of true existence. It is a mind that perversely or wrongly misconceives its object. Therefore, by cultivating an unmistaken understanding as its antidote we can eliminate it.

Both the ignorance that is a misconception of true existence and its antidote depend on causes and conditions. They are alike in that they grow when in contact with favorable conditions and cease to exist when confronted by adverse factors. We may ask, what are the differences between the two? Since the ignorance that is a misconception of true existence is a mind that is wrong with respect to its object, it cannot develop limitlessly. This is because it does not have a valid support. This mind is wrong, or perverse, in the sense that the way it conceives the object is contrary to the actual way the object exists. The mind perceiving selflessness is an antidote, or opponent, to this and is not mistaken with respect to its object. That is to say, it is correct with respect to its object, which means that the way it perceives its object conforms to the way the object actually exists. Because it is not a wrong perception, it has a valid basis of support.

It was earlier stated that the ignorance that is a misconception of true existence could be brought to an end. This is because the ignorant mind does not have the support of being a valid cognition. On the other hand, the mind that perceives the selfless nature of an object does have the support of being a valid cognition. The ways these two minds perceive objects are in direct contradiction. The mind that perceives the selfless nature of an object is a powerful antidote against that ignorant mind, and therefore the ignorant mind can be overcome. This is analogous to the way in which any aspect of human misery can be reduced when the appropriate measures are applied to counter it. It is in the nature of things that their potential is reduced when confronted by opposing factors.

The mind that perceives reality is referred to as transcendental awareness and is a positive quality of the mind. It has the support of being a valid cognition. It is in the nature of the mind that when you habituate it with a positive quality it can be developed limitlessly. Unlike the mind, the positive qualities of the body do not have this quality of being able to expand to a limitless extent. This is due simply to the fact that the body is composed of gross elements, and attributes of such gross form do not have the potential to expand limitlessly.

When we say that the ignorant mind is perverse or wrong, we are talking about the way it misconceives reality. Now the pertinent questions are: What is reality? How is this mind mistaken about reality? And in what way does the mind wrongly apprehend reality? Reality or emptiness of true existence is something that can be established logically. There are sound, or perfect, reasons to prove the emptiness of inherent existence, and we can gain conviction in these reasons. On the other hand, there is no logical way to prove true existence. True existence is what appears to an ordinary, untrained consciousness. But when it comes under logical scrutiny, true existence cannot be found. Even in our everyday life we often find contradictions between the way certain things appear and their actual mode of existence; that is, the way things actually exist is different from the way they appear to exist. This notion can be illustrated quite simply: in worldly affairs, we talk about somebody being let down or disillusioned. Disillusionment arises due to a discrepancy between the way a situation appears to be and the way it actually is.

Let us examine our situation as human beings. Compared to animals, our minds are immensely more powerful. We have the ability to analyze whether there is a reality beyond the level of appearance, whereas animals only deal with what appears to them. This is very clear, just as different people have different mental capacities. When we closely examine them, many of the minds that are generally understood as valid cognizers are also mistaken in a deeper sense. The way phenomena really exist is other than what appears to such minds. We normally perceive reality or emptiness as existing differently from the way it actually exists. Our perception of impermanent things like mountain ranges and houses does not conform to their actual mode of existence. Some of these things have existed for many centuries, even thousands of years. And our minds perceive them in just that way—as lasting and permanent, impervious to momentary change. Yet when we examine these objects on an atomic level, they disintegrate every moment; they undergo momentary change. Science also describes a similar pattern of change. These objects appear solid, stable, and lasting, but in their true nature, they constantly change, not keeping still even for a moment.

Chapter 2

Training the Mind

It is essential to study and acquire an education. Training the mind is a process of familiarization. In the Buddhist context, familiarization, or meditation, refers to the positive transformation of the mind, that is, to the elimination of its defective qualities and the improvement of its positive qualities. Through meditation we can train our minds in such a way that negative qualities are abandoned and positive qualities are generated and enhanced. In general we talk about two types of meditation: analytical and single-pointed. First, the object of meditation is put through a process of analysis in which one repeatedly attempts to gain familiarity with the subject matter. When the practitioner has gained a good deal of certainty about the object of meditation, the mind is made to concentrate on it without further analysis. The combination of analytical and concentrative meditation is an effective technique to familiarize the mind with the object of meditation, and thus helps to train the mind properly.

We must recognize the importance of training the mind. It arises from the fundamental fact that each and every one of us innately desires happiness and does not want misery. These are natural human characteristics that don't have to be created. This desire is not wrong. The question is, how do we achieve these objectives of realizing happiness and relinquishing misery? The basic purpose of education, for instance, is to gain happiness and avoid misery. Individuals struggle through the process of education so that they can enjoy a successful and meaningful life. With education we can increase happiness and reduce misery. Education takes various forms; nevertheless, all of them are essentially intended to help train and shape the mind. The mind has power over the body and speech, and therefore any training of body and speech must begin with the mind. Put in another way, for any physical or verbal training to take place, there must first be a motivation. The mind sees the advantages of such training and generates interest in it. The purpose of training the mind is to make our lives worthwhile. Through the process of training the mind we learn many new things, and we are also able to detect and identify numerous defects or things that can be removed or corrected. Now the task we face is to discover the means and methods that can enable us to eliminate what is wrong and assemble favorable conditions for transforming our minds. This is crucial. In our everyday life, education helps us to find the necessary and conducive factors that give rise to happiness. In the process, we are also able to abandon the factors that make us miserable. Thus, through education, we aim to make our lives happy and worthwhile.

When we look at our lives within a social context, education has a vital role to play. How we fare in any given situation depends on the conduct of our body, speech, and mind. Since mind is the chief, a disciplined mind is essential. Happiness or sorrow in life depend on the power or intelligence of the mind. And how these experiences affect our lives also depends on the mind. The conduct of our body, speech, and mind now can also determine our state of being in the future. This in turn depends on the cast of our minds. When we misuse our mental potential, we make mistakes and suffer unpleasant consequences. On the other hand, when the mind's potential is skillfully harnessed, we derive positive and pleasant results. Our state of mind and how the mind perceives different things greatly affects us. Because of the control they have over their minds, some people are little disturbed by failure or adverse circumstances. This is a clear example of why taming, or training, the mind is so important.

Having considered the importance of training the mind, we might wonder what the mind is. If you ask them, most people respond by rubbing their heads and then pointing to their brains. This is partly correct, because we are talking specifically about the human mind. The human mind does not have any existence independent of the human body. The consciousness that has a particular relation to the human body is referred to as a human consciousness. And the consciousness that has a particular relation with an animal body is referred to as an animal consciousness. The human mind, or consciousness, we are talking about actually consists of a vast number of minds, some subtle and some coarse. Many of the coarser types are connected to a sense organ like the eye, and many of them are definitely connected to the brain. It is obvious that these external bases, or factors, are essential for a consciousness to arise. But the main cause of any mind is the preceding moment of consciousness, whose nature is clarity and awareness. This is referred to as the immediate condition.

The *Four Hundred Verses* by Aryadeva mentions the logical requirement that a root cause of consciousness must have the potential to transform and have a nature of clarity and awareness. Otherwise, consciousness would either never be produced, or it would be produced at all times, which is obviously not acceptable. The impact of an action is left on our mental consciousness, and as a result we can recall the experience after a month or a year, or even after ten years or more. This is what is known as awakening a latent potency. This potency has been passed on through the continuity of consciousness, and when the necessary conditions come into play, the past latent imprint comes to the surface. Thus, we talk about awakening latent imprints from previous lives. However, the mind's relation to the brain cannot sufficiently describe the subtle aspects of a latent potency. Understanding of this notion of latent potency can help us gain some appreciation for life and the formation and disintegration of the universe. It can also answer certain doubts concerning our human thoughts, superstitions, and other projections of the mind.

Buddhist philosophy very clearly describes the guidelines and the methods by which it is possible to obtain an omniscient mind, the highest quality of mind representing the full consummation of its potential and power. In order to realize the final fruit of the omniscient mind, we need to train in its complete and correct causes. We must also ensure that we maintain the proper sequence of training. This is why the text states:

> **Also from among these causes and conditions, you should cultivate correct and complete causes. If you put the wrong causes into practice, even if you work hard for a long time, the desired goal cannot be achieved. It will be like milking a [cow's] horn. Likewise, the result will not be produced when all the causes are not put into effect. For example, if the seed or any other cause is missing, then the result, a sprout, and so forth, will not be produced. Therefore, those who desire a particular result should cultivate its complete and unmistaken causes and conditions.**

Besides assembling complete and correct causes, it is essential to train in the right sequence of causes for the mind to expand and become omniscient. For example, in order to prepare a delicious meal, the mere collection of all the necessary ingredients is not enough. We need to know how to assemble the different ingredients like oil, spices, and so forth, in order to achieve the desired flavor.

> **If you ask, "What are the causes and conditions of the final fruit of omniscience?" I, who am like a blind man, may not be in a position to explain [by myself], but I shall employ the Buddha's own words just as he spoke them to his disciples after his enlightenment. He said, "Vajrapani, Lord of Secrets, the transcendental wisdom of omniscience has its root in compassion, and arises**

> **from a cause—the altruistic thought, the awakening mind of bodhichitta, and the perfection of skillful means." Therefore, if you are interested in achieving omniscience, you need to practice these three: compassion, the awakening mind of bodhichitta, and skillful means.**

Here, Kamalashila refers to the words of the Buddha and establishes the correct causes and means to achieve omniscience. He says that anyone interested in omniscience should practice the awakening mind of bodhichitta, which is based on compassion. The practice should be supported by the six perfections, with special emphasis on the union of calm abiding meditation and special insight. Therefore, the aspects of practice known as method and wisdom should be seen as so complementary that they are regarded as inseparable. This also implies that compassion is the root of the Buddha's doctrine, and that the entire body of teachings contained in both the greater and lesser vehicles is based on compassion.

Chapter 3

Compassion

Moved by compassion, Bodhisattvas take the vow to liberate all sentient beings.

Compassion is essential in the initial stage, in the intermediate stage, and in the final stage of spiritual development. In accordance with this popular teaching, Bodhisattvas, great beings who are strongly motivated and moved by compassion, pledge to attain the state of omniscience for the welfare of all sentient beings. This determination is the awakening mind of bodhichitta, which is an altruistic thought, derived from compassion.

Then by overcoming their self-centered outlook, they engage eagerly and continuously in the very difficult practices of accumulating merit and insight.

By the power of generating the awakening mind of bodhichitta, they undergo the Bodhisattvas' training, which includes developing the six perfections, without questioning how long it will take to fulfill it. As a result they are gradually able to accumulate immense merit and insight without much effort.

> **Having entered into this practice, they will certainly complete the collection of merit and insight. Accomplishing the accumulation of merit and insight is like having omniscience itself in the palm of your hand. Therefore, since compassion is the only root of omniscience, you should become familiar with this practice from the very beginning.**

Here the author mentions that compassion is the *only* root, or foundation, of omniscience. The word "only" stresses that compassion is an essential cause of omniscience, but does not negate other causes and conditions. It emphasizes the point that compassion is a necessary cause because omniscience cannot be achieved without compassion. If compassion alone were sufficient, then the earlier statement about the need to train in compassion, the awakening mind of bodhichitta, and skillful means would be contradicted.

> **The *Compendium of Perfect Dharma* reads, "O Buddha, a Bodhisattva should not train in many practices. If a Bodhisattva properly holds to one Dharma and learns it perfectly, he has all the Buddha's qualities in the palm of his hand. And, if you ask what that one Dharma is, it is great compassion."**

Here the Buddha strongly emphasizes the importance of compassion. It is on the basis of compassion that the awakening mind of bodhichitta is generated, and the individual engages in the deeds of a Bodhisattva and so attains enlightenment. The corollary of the thesis is that without compassion, you cannot generate the supreme awakening mind of bodhichitta that cherishes others more than yourself. Without this altruistic attitude it is impossible to practice the Mahayana deeds of Bodhisattvas such as the six perfections. And without following this procedure, you cannot achieve the omniscient state of Buddhahood. This is why compassion is so important.

> **The Buddhas have already achieved all their own goals, but remain in the cycle of existence for as long as there are sentient beings. This is because they possess great compassion. They also do not enter the immensely blissful abode of nirvana like the Hearers. Considering the interests of sentient beings first, they abandon the peaceful abode of nirvana as if it were a burning iron house. Therefore, great compassion alone is the unavoidable cause of the non-abiding nirvana of the Buddha.**

Compassion is highly commended in many treatises, and its importance cannot be overemphasized. Chandrakirti paid rich tribute to compassion, saying that it was essential in the initial, intermediate, and final stages of the path to enlightenment.

Initially, the awakening mind of bodhichitta is generated with compassion as the root, or basis. Practice of the six perfections and so forth is essential if a Bodhisattva is to attain the final goal. In the intermediate stage, compassion is equally relevant. Even after enlightenment, it is compassion that induces the Buddhas not to abide in the blissful state of complacent nirvana. It is the motivating force enabling the Buddhas to enter non-abiding nirvana and actualize the Truth Body, which represents fulfillment of your own purpose, and the Form Body, which represents fulfillment of the needs of others. Thus, by the power of compassion, Buddhas serve the interests of sentient beings without interruption for as long as space exists. This shows that the awakening mind of bodhichitta remains crucial even after achieving the final destination. Kamalashila's reference to another treatise by Chandrakirti supports the validity of this thesis and also has the advantage of helping to persuade his audience.

Generally, in the Buddhist tradition, philosophical views do not have to be proved by scriptural authority alone. In fact, individuals must rely primarily on logic and reasoning to gain faith and conviction in the philosophy. Objects of knowledge can be broadly classified as obvious phenomena, partially concealed phenomena, and completely concealed phenomena. There is no need to use logic to prove the existence of obvious phenomena. We can experience and understand them directly and thus ascertain their existence. Since partially concealed phenomena cannot be ascertained through direct experience, they need to be established by applying logic. The object of analysis is then understood by inferential cognition based on experience. Several lines of reasoning may be necessary to achieve the purpose. People whose understanding is of an initial level of development cannot possibly examine completely concealed phenomena through the science of logic. Such phenomena can hardly be established in relation to our experience either. This is where we have to rely on valid scriptural authority.

The reliability, or authority, of scriptural teachings needs to be established first. Likewise, the validity, or credibility, of the teacher who gave such teachings must be proven. Scriptural authority must be able to withstand a three-tier analysis—that teachings concerning obvious phenomena are not contradicted by direct apprehension; that teachings concerning partially obscure phenomena are not contradicted by inferential cognition; and that its teachings concerning very obscure phenomena are not contradicted by inferential cognition based on faith. The validity of such scriptural authority in turn should be tested by logical reasoning.

As it is taught that the teachings are true, or valid, in relation to the main meaning, or the chief goal, their validity concerning other goals can be understood by inference. Our chief goal is the state of definite goodness (nirvana and omniscience), while favorable rebirth as a human being or god is an ordinary goal. So when teachings that propound the process for realizing definite goodness are not found to be faulty under logical examination, it is simply not possible for them to be faulty with regard to the ordinary goal. It is a matter of common sense that when something is true with respect to the difficult aspects of a question, its being true concerning simple matters is beyond doubt.

Furthermore, the teacher who gave these teachings was an honorable and dependable person. He gained his realization through the power of his practice of compassion. Because he possessed great compassion, he was truly motivated to benefit all sentient beings. By the force of great compassion, he gave the teachings in order to demonstrate the course of the path that helped him to eliminate the obstacles and transcend to the state of highest perfection. The Buddha taught in the light of his own experience, and since he had direct realization of ultimate reality he was extremely proficient in revealing the truth. His service was unconditional and tireless, and he was prepared to work in the interest of sentient beings for eons irrespective of the nature of the task involved. Understanding and reflecting on these points should help us gain conviction in the validity of his teachings.

For these reasons, it is said to be wise to cite certain textual teachings to substantiate a thesis or a practice. Such a process has a great purpose—it dispels numerous unwarranted doubts and instills new insights.

Chapter 4

Developing Equanimity, the Root of Loving-Kindness

Compassion is one of the major causes for realizing the state of omniscience. It is important at the beginning of the practice, during the practice, and even after realizing the results of our spiritual endeavor. Now the question is: How should we meditate on it?

> **The way to meditate on compassion will be taught from the outset. Begin the practice by meditating on equanimity. Try to actualize impartiality toward all sentient beings by eliminating attachment and hatred.**

Compassion is a mind that focuses on the sentient beings that are miserable and wishes them to be free from suffering. Compassion can be of three types, depending on the aspect of wisdom that accompanies it. These three are: compassion focused on sentient beings, compassion focused on phenomena, and compassion focused on the unapprehendable. All three are the same in being minds that earnestly desire sentient beings to be free from their misery. They are distinguished not in terms of their aspect, but in terms of their object of focus, because all three have the same aspect of wishing sentient beings to be separated from suffering. Compassion focused on sentient beings is so-called because it focuses merely on sentient beings without specifying their characteristics of being impermanent or empty of inherent existence. Compassion focused on phenomena refers to that compassion which not only focuses on sentient beings, but also focuses on sentient beings characterized by impermanence. Likewise, compassion focused on the unapprehendable refers to that compassion which focuses on sentient beings characterized by the unapprehendable, or their lack of inherent existence.

When we look at it from another angle, the merit of generating a kind thought is obvious. This is true whether you believe in a particular religion or not. A person's general goodness is in direct correlation to the force, or quality, of the kind thoughts he or she generates. A kind person finds a lot of admirers, and they feel close to such a person. We can observe this phenomenon even among animals. Animals exhibit great joy and delight when they see people who are kind to them. And they enjoy being around such persons. Conversely, people who are aggressive and hold evil designs are regarded with suspicion even by animals and birds. Animals and birds run away when they hear their voices or even their footsteps. Therefore, a kind motivation or a kind heart is an extremely valuable quality.

People who possess compassion are amiable to all and their pleasing nature attracts friends everywhere. It is easy to observe the attraction of their compassionate motivation when we notice even strangers taking delight in their company. Let us take some simple examples that clearly illustrate the meaning of kindness. For instance, when someone smiles, it creates joy in other people's hearts without costing anything. Unless we are peaceful and joyful at heart, we will have no guarantee of winning friends, even if we possess great wealth. When we are competitive and aggressive, it is hard to gain much substantial benefit even if we lavish wealth on others. On the other hand those who are sincerely interested in helping others have peace and joy at heart. They create an atmosphere of harmony around them. Thus it should be clear that a kind heart and a helpful attitude are the very foundation of happiness, both for others and ourselves for now and forever.

The positive qualities produced by helpful intentions are widely recognized as worthwhile and desirable. All the major religions of the world teach their followers to become good people, to practice patience, and to develop an interest in helping others. There is unanimity concerning the positive value attached to these fundamental principles. In Buddhism particularly, since its doctrine is based on compassion, a great deal of emphasis is placed on this practice.

So, what is the Buddhist technique for meditating on compassion? On the one hand we need to develop loving-kindness toward suffering beings, and secondly we must identify the nature of suffering. Maintaining awareness of these two points, and focusing your mind on the infinite number of beings, you will be able to generate a strong wish that all of them gain freedom from suffering and its causes. You should begin the process by attempting to develop loving-kindness toward beings who are in misery. For this purpose, meditation on equanimity is taught.

If we examine the state of our ordinary minds, we may see how they segregate sentient beings into three groups—those to whom we feel close, those for whom we feel aversion, and those toward whom we are indifferent. We regard certain beings as close friends and relatives. We hold others at a distance, with the thought that they have harmed us, our friends, relatives, and possessions in the past, that they do it now, and will do the same thing in the future. With thoughts like these, we generate aversion toward those beings. Under such circumstances, even if we talk about cultivating compassion for all beings, in reality, as far as our own purposes are concerned, our compassion toward others is one sided and superficial. Therefore, in order to generate true compassion for all beings, we must first develop an attitude of equanimity, an impartial thought that views all sentient beings equally.

It is also important to recognize that, although we feel close to our friends and relatives and are generally kind to them, this particular kindness springs from attachment and grasping. A selfish motive is behind our apparent kindness. We are biased, thinking that this person has benefited me in this way or that person related to me in that way. So when we use the term "kindness" in everyday terms, we refer to something that would more accurately be called attachment.

What do we mean when we speak of a truly compassionate kindness? Compassion is essentially concern for others' welfare—their happiness and their suffering. Others wish to avoid misery as much as we do. So a compassionate person feels concerned when others are miserable and develops a positive intention to free them from it. As ordinary beings, our feeling of closeness to our friends and relatives is little more than an expression of clinging desire. It needs to be tempered, not enhanced. It is important not to confuse attachment and compassion. In some texts, the term "attachment" is used to denote compassion. Though attachment shares some similarity with compassion, it is produced in dependence on the misconception of true existence. Compassion, on the other hand, does not necessarily depend on the misconception of true existence. A compassionate thought is motivated by a wish to help release beings from their misery.

Broadly there are two major techniques for developing equanimity. According to the first, we think about the uncertainty of relationships, and about impermanence, and suffering, and come to see the futility of clinging to some people and hating others. According to the second technique, seeing that all beings are the same in terms of wishing to gain happiness and to be free of suffering, we try to develop an impartial attitude toward all beings. The root text briefly summarizes this second method for developing equanimity:

> **All sentient beings desire happiness and do not desire misery. Think deeply about how, in this beginningless cycle of existence, there is not one sentient being who has not been my friend and relative hundreds of**

> **times. Therefore, since there is no ground for being attached to some and hating others, I shall develop a mind of equanimity toward all sentient beings. Begin the meditation on equanimity by thinking of a neutral person, and then consider people who are friends and foes.**

All sentient beings are exactly the same in that every one desires happiness and seeks to avoid misery. We are not isolated entities disconnected from each other. The happiness and suffering of other beings affect us. This mutual relation is obvious. Sentient beings have been kind and have benefited us directly and indirectly throughout beginningless time. These beings are intrinsically the same as us in their pursuit of happiness and effort to avoid suffering. Thus, it is essentially logical for us to train in cultivating an impartial attitude wishing for the happiness of all beings.

In order to actualize a state of mind that regards everyone equally, at times it can be more effective to meditate on particular individuals. Visualize three individuals: one who has done us harm in this life, our enemy; one who has benefited us directly, our friend; and one who has neither harmed nor benefited us, a stranger.

When we examine the mind's usual automatic response, we note that regarding the enemy, the mind thinks, "This is my foe." It becomes irritated and resentful or hateful. Thinking about the friend, the mind feels relaxed and comfortable. Toward the stranger, there is neither irritation nor feelings of delight. The next step is to look for the reasons for these types of responses. The reasons are in fact superficial and based on narrow, self-serving attitudes. We are attached to friends and relatives because of the temporary benefit they have brought us in this life. We hate our enemies because of some harm they have inflicted on us. People are not our friends from birth, but become so due to circumstances. Neither were our enemies born hostile. Such relationships are not at all reliable. In the course of our lives, our best friend today can turn out to be our worst enemy tomorrow. And a much-hated enemy can change into our most trusted friend. Moreover, if we talk about our many lives in the past, the unreliability of this relationship is all the more apparent. For these reasons, our animosity toward enemies and attachment toward friends merely exhibits a narrow-minded attitude that can only see some temporary and fleeting advantage. On the contrary, when we view things from a broader perspective with more farsightedness, equanimity will dawn in our minds, enabling us to see the futility of hostility and clinging desire.

When, through prolonged meditation, we are able to equalize our feelings toward those three individuals—the friend, foe, and stranger—gradually extend the scope of the meditation to our neighbors, our fellow citizens, and our compatriots. Eventually, we extend the meditation to include all the beings in the world. Starting with specific individuals is an effective way to develop perfect equanimity. If we initially meditate on a vast number of beings, our practice of equanimity may appear to be fairly sound, but when we are confronted by specific individuals we will realize how little ground we have gained. For this reason the technique of gradually expanding the scope of our meditation is praised and recommended by many masters of the past.

Let us consider the concept of the beginningless cycle of existence. It may be described on one level as a continual cyclic process from one instant to the next under the influence of disturbing emotions and karma. This situation has its causes, but the causes are not permanent. If the causes were permanent, the result would have to be permanent. Neither is the cycle of existence a product of the intention of Ishvara, whom some believe to be the creator. So what is the cycle of existence? It comes into existence sharing the essential nature of its causes. The two root causes for being born in the cycle of existence are karma and disturbing emotions, with the latter dominating. The ignorance that is a misconception of true existence is the most serious among the three principal disturbing emotions. Ignorance that is a misconception of true existence is not something imported from elsewhere, but is a creation of consciousness.

The natural thing to do is to investigate whether consciousness exists or not. It may be difficult to come to any definite conclusions, and we may have to limit ourselves to saying it exists in the nature of things. However, the ignorance which is at the root of all the other disturbing emotions and which is a cause for birth in the cycle of existence comes into existence at the same instant as consciousness. And consciousness has no beginning. If we were to assert that consciousness does have a beginning, numerous fallacies would ensue. If, for example, we accept an inanimate physical entity as consciousness's starting point, by implication we are accepting results from inappropriate causes.

In normal cause and effect relations, both cause and effect are of the same category. When we observe the cause and effect relations of physical objects, the result maintains intrinsically the same nature as its cause. Consciousness too follows a similar pattern. Every moment of consciousness produces a subsequent result of the same category, that is, another moment of consciousness. For these reasons, Buddhist scriptural texts expound the notion of beginningless mind and the beginningless existence of sentient beings. Thus, the cycle of existence is said to have no beginning.

The text mentions that in the course of being born in this beginningless cycle of existence, sentient beings have been our relatives countless times. Here we need to recall and reflect on the kindness of sentient beings. Every one of them has benefited us directly or indirectly. The kindness and benefit rendered by our friends and relatives of this life are quite obvious. Even strangers are of immense value as a basis for accumulating merit. Loving-kindness and compassion are cultivated in relation to the infinite number of sentient beings by remembering their kindness to us.

As an outcome of these practices, the awakening mind of bodhichitta is generated. Thus, the training to accumulate merit and wisdom is done in relation to sentient beings and we are enormously benefited. Therefore, we depend on the kindness of sentient beings to achieve the final unsurpassed goal. It is from this perspective that the *Guide to the Bodhisattva's Way of Life* by Shantideva explains that sentient beings and Buddhas are equal in terms of their helping individuals attain the state of Buddhahood. Sentient beings are of immense value and help, regardless of their intentions. On a mundane conventional level, enemies are those who cause us harm, and we are hostile to them for doing so. But, viewed in another light, we can gain great experience and training from our relationships with our enemies. It is in relation to enemies that we can primarily practice patience and tolerance and thus reduce the burden of anger and hatred. We should take maximum advantage of this opportunity to enrich and enhance our practice of patience. It is for reasons like these that some treatises describe our enemies as our best teachers. In short, all sentient beings, including our enemies, give us great help in various ways and directly or indirectly render us much-needed service.

> **After the mind has developed equanimity toward all sentient beings, meditate on loving-kindness. Moisten the mental continuum with the water of loving-kindness and prepare it as you would a piece of fertile ground. When the seed of compassion is planted in such a mind, germination will be swift, proper, and complete. Once you have irrigated the mindstream with loving-kindness, meditate on compassion.**

To illustrate the way to generate benevolence and compassion, Kamalashila draws an analogy with the cultivation of crops. Just as a seed will grow if you plant it in ground moistened with water, you can cultivate compassion when you have prepared the mind with thoughts of loving-kindness as the basis. Having cultivated equanimity toward all sentient beings, we should see all sentient beings as similar in having been our close friends and relatives in many lives, and as similar to us in desiring happiness and disliking suffering. Having trained your mind in this way, you will feel very close to all beings and develop great empathy for them. The more an individual finds sentient beings attractive and dear to his or her heart, the more he or she will be concerned about their misery and pain. Therefore, having meditated on equanimity, we should meditate on loving-kindness. Having moistened our mind with the water of loving-kindness, if we plant the seed of compassion in it, its growth will be swift and smooth.

Chapter 5

Identifying the Nature of Suffering

The compassionate mind has the nature of wishing all suffering beings to be free from suffering. Meditate on compassion for all sentient beings, because the beings in the three realms of existence are intensely tortured by the three types of sufferings in various forms. The Buddha has said that heat and other types of pain constantly torture beings in the hells for a very long time. He has also said that hungry ghosts are scorched by hunger and thirst and experience immense physical suffering. We can also see animals suffering in many miserable ways: they eat each other, become angry, and are hurt and killed. We can see that human beings, too, experience various acute kinds of pain. Not able to find what they want, they are resentful and harm each other. They suffer the pain of losing the beautiful things they want and confronting the ugly things they do not want, as well as the pain of poverty.

After establishing the process of training by which we learn to see suffering sentient beings as lovable and attractive, Kamalashila deals with the various types of miseries that torture them. The three types of misery are the misery of suffering, the misery of change, and pervasive misery. There is not one sentient being who is not tortured by each of them. Sentient beings in the three higher realms in the cycle of existence may enjoy temporary contaminated happiness or some neutral feelings, but in the final analysis, they are under the influence of pervasive misery. And as such, they are worthy of compassion. Kamalashila has also briefly referred to the sufferings of the beings in the hells, the hungry ghosts, animals, and human beings. He further points out some of the unique causes that make human beings miserable:

> **There are those whose minds are bound by various fetters of disturbing emotions like craving desire. Others are in turmoil with different types of wrong views. These are all causes of misery; therefore they are always painful, like being on a precipice.**

Gods too have different miseries:

> **Gods suffer the misery of change. For example, signs of impending death and their fall to unfortunate states constantly oppress the minds of gods of the desire realm. How can they live in peace?**

The text now defines pervasive misery:

> **Pervasive misery is what arises under the power of causes characterized by actions and disturbing emotions. It has the nature and characteristics of momentary disintegration and pervades all wandering beings.**

The misery of suffering refers to what we usually recognize as suffering, physical pain, sickness, and mental anxiety. What we usually recognize as happiness (that is, contaminated or impure happiness) is characterized as the misery of change. Contaminated happiness is not perfect happiness, but rather the mere absence of the grosser kinds of suffering. Since contaminated happiness does not last, but is brought to an end by unpleasantness, it is characterized as the misery of change. Pervasive misery refers to sentient beings' collection of mental and physical constituents, known as the contaminated aggregates, which result from past karma and disturbing emotions, and act as an agent to generate further karma and disturbing emotions. There may be occasions when we are disturbed by neither the misery of suffering nor the misery of change. But as long as we are not separated from our contaminated mental and physical aggregates, they will continue to provide the basis for various kinds of misery. And when they come into contact with the appropriate factors and conditions, suffering is bound to arise. Therefore, it is essential to think about these three types of misery.

The next step in this process of mental training concerns the will to be free from such misery. It is crucial that we identify the true nature of these sufferings in order to generate a desire to be free of them. Even animals understand the misery of suffering as unbearable and wish to be free from it. Both Buddhists and non-Buddhists who seek the qualities of higher realms, like those of the higher levels of concentration and the formless world, understand the misery of change as unpleasant. They are able to free themselves temporarily from the misery of suffering. When they reach such higher realms, like those below the fourth level of concentration, where there is only the feeling of neutrality, they are temporarily free from the misery of change. Those in the fourth meditative stage and in the formless realms are temporarily free from the first two types of miseries. Recognizing pervasive misery is the catalyst that stimulates individuals to seek the state of liberation. When they apprehend its true identity, they generate a sense of disgust. They become aware of the disadvantages of disturbing emotions and their instability. Understanding the flaws of the disturbing emotions must precede understanding the flaws of the contaminated mental and physical aggregates. Seeing the flaws, or drawbacks, of the disturbing emotions provokes us to try to part from them. When we eliminate our disturbing emotions, we gain what is known as nirvana, or liberation. Proper identification of pervasive suffering and a strong dislike for it are the determining factors in the process of developing true renunciation, or the will to gain liberation.

The text has mentioned the momentary nature of pervasive suffering. This concept can be interpreted in two ways, which can be illustrated by an example. Firstly, anything impermanent disintegrates and changes every moment. For instance, an omniscient mind is impermanent, and it too shares the same nature of disintegrating moment by moment. Secondly, an impermanent phenomenon has no independent identity and is under the influence of other factors like its causes and conditions. As such, pervasive suffering does not remain constant even for a moment, but is in a steady process of disintegration and change.

> **Therefore, see all wandering beings as immersed in a great fire of misery. Think that they are all like you in**

> **not desiring misery at all: "Alas! All my beloved sentient beings are in such pain. What can I do to set them free?" and make their sufferings your own. Whether you are engaged in one-pointed meditation or pursuing your ordinary activities, meditate on compassion at all times, focusing on all sentient beings and wishing that they all be free from suffering.**
>
> **Begin by meditating on your friends and relatives. Recognize how they experience the various sufferings that have been explained.**

In the preceding lines, the author outlines the steps of meditation on compassion. Compassion is the wish that all sentient beings be free from suffering and its causes. In order to train the mind to be compassionate, you must maintain a practice that includes both formal meditation sessions and awareness during the period that follows. That is, not only should a practitioner train to generate a compassionate mind during formal meditation, but also during activities like walking, sleeping, sitting, working, and so forth. If you can maintain such a program, you will be able to make good use of the different experiences you have during the post-meditation period, which will enhance your development of a compassionate mind. On the other hand, if you do not cultivate awareness and mindfulness during the post-meditation periods and you let your mind wander, the progress of your meditation will be slowed. This is definitely a fault to be corrected. You must try to retain the flavor, or essence, of your meditation as you go about your other activities. This will greatly aid the progress of your realizations during the session, and those realizations in turn will contribute to your spiritual development during the post-meditation period. This is how you can enjoy a stream of meritorious energy.

> **Then having seen all sentient beings as equal, with no difference between them, you should meditate on sentient beings to whom you are indifferent. When the compassion you feel toward them is the same as the compassion you feel toward your friends and relatives, meditate on compassion for all sentient beings throughout the ten directions of the universe.**

When you are meditating on compassion, if you specifically focus on a sentient being who is experiencing suffering, as we did during our meditation on equanimity, your meditation on compassion will be more effective. Initially, you can visualize the intense suffering of beings in the unfortunate realms. You can also meditate on compassion for those who are indulging in forceful negative actions, which possess the three factors of intention, action and, completion. Although they may not presently be experiencing great misery, they are accumulating powerful causes to experience it later. If you meditate along these lines, it will greatly help you train your mind to become compassionate toward each and every sentient being in the cycle of existence—all of them are under the sway of disturbing emotions, slaves to the ignorance that is a misconception of true existence and self-centeredness.

Kamalashila speaks of all sentient beings as being equal. This can be interpreted in two ways: ultimately and conventionally. The equality of beings on an ultimate level does not obviate the existence of friends and foes on the conventional level. However, when your meditation focuses on the unfindability of objects on an ultimate level, it counteracts attachment and hatred by countering the misconception of true existence.

These are some of the many techniques by which we train to develop an even-minded attitude. It is important to maintain this kind of meditational procedure and accumulate the positive potential of merit. Eventually our ordinary compassion toward miserable beings can be enhanced and transformed into a more purified state. The compassion we feel at present is usually mixed with attachment. But the presence of this compassion also indicates that we have the basis for true compassion. Occasionally we also generate spontaneous compassion toward strangers in great pain, wondering what we can do to alleviate their suffering. This is an expression of our innate compassion. It is crucial that we recognize this fact, cherish this compassionate thought, and then promote and enhance it. If you do not possess this innate compassion, try to cultivate it and make every effort to develop it. In due course, such compassion, however insignificant it may seem to be at present, can expand infinitely.

The text now explains the measure of having cultivated such compassion.

> **Just as a mother responds to her small, beloved, and suffering child, when you develop a spontaneous and equal sense of compassion toward all sentient beings, you have perfected the practice of compassion. And this is known as great compassion.**

In the depths of your heart you have great care and concern for your beloved child whatever you are doing, whether you are walking, sitting, or talking. If you are able to cultivate such a mind toward all infinite sentient beings, thinking how good it would be if they were free from suffering, and if such a mind arises automatically, without your needing to rely on special reasons, that is an indication that you have cultivated genuine great compassion.

Whatever realizations you want to cultivate, you must first know what the object of your attention is and what causes and conditions you need to cultivate to be able to generate such a realization. You need to do some preparation. Having gained familiarity and some experience in such a process of practice, you may not need to cultivate any additional understanding. But using analysis and investigation, you should cultivate a strong feeling within that really moves your mind. That is called actual experience and it is of two kinds: contrived experience and uncontrived experience. Contrived experience refers to those feelings that arise within your mind as a result of using subtle reasons and depending on quotations from the scriptures. When you do not engage in analysis and investigation, you do not get such experience. After having cultivated such a contrived experience, if you continue the process of strengthening and developing it, a time will come when you encounter a particular situation such that, without having to rely on a quotation or a reason, a strong feeling automatically arises within your mind. That is called uncontrived experience. When you achieve such an uncontrived experience of compassion, that is an indication of having cultivated a genuine great compassion.

Then the text discusses the process of meditation on loving-kindness. The measure of having cultivated loving-kindness is similar to the measure of having cultivated great compassion. Compassion is a mind wishing that sentient beings be free from suffering, and loving-kindness is a mind wishing that they meet with happiness. Loving-kindness induces compassion, and compassion induces the special attitude. The special attitude here means that you not only mentally think how good it would be if sentient beings were free from suffering, but you voluntarily take responsibility for actually engaging in the work of delivering sentient beings to the state of liberation and helping them remove their sufferings. And this induces the awakening mind of bodhichitta.

> **Meditation on loving-kindness begins with friends and people you are fond of. It has the nature of wishing that they meet with happiness. Gradually extend the meditation to include strangers and even your enemies. Habituating yourself to compassion, you will gradually generate a spontaneous wish to liberate all sentient beings. Therefore, having familiarized yourself with compassion as the basis, meditate on the awakening mind of bodhichitta.**
>
> **Bodhichitta is of two types: conventional and ultimate. Conventional bodhichitta is the cultivation of the initial thought that aspires to attain unsurpassable and perfectly consummated Buddhahood in order to benefit all wandering sentient beings, after having taken the vow out of compassion to release all of them**

> **from suffering. That conventional bodhichitta should be cultivated in a process similar to that described in the chapter on moral ethics in the *Bodhisattvabhumi*, generating this mind by taking the Bodhisattva vow before a master who abides by the Bodhisattva precepts.**

The measure of your cultivation of the awakening mind of bodhichitta is similar to the cultivation of compassion. First you cultivate bodhichitta as a contrived experience, then you cultivate the awakening mind of bodhichitta as an uncontrived experience, which is the state of the genuine awakening mind of bodhichitta.

The great Indian master Shantideva has said that all the sufferings we see in the world arise because we are so self-centered, because we wish only for our own personal happiness. All the happiness we see in this world arises because of our taking care of the welfare of other sentient beings. He says that there is no need to elaborate further on this point. If you examine the difference between the state of the Buddha and an ordinary being, it will be easily understood. The Buddha worked for the benefit of other sentient beings, achieved omniscience, and now has the capacity to benefit all sentient beings, whereas we ordinary sentient beings, even though we have tried our best to fulfill our personal well-being, because of our self-centered attitude not only have not achieved omniscience, but we are still in the cycle of existence. Even in the case of the achievement of nirvana, if we pursue it mainly out of self-interest, it will be just solitary liberation or liberation without omniscience. This is also due to the self-centered attitude. Even on a day-to-day basis, all good qualities within this world such as feeling mentally at ease, having many trusted friends and relatives, and living in a place where you are not deceived by others, are the result of concern for others' welfare. And ultimately the possibility of achieving enlightenment is also due to this mind.

In other words, if we compare ourselves with the Buddha and calculate how many faults we have and how many perfect qualities a Buddha has, we will be able to discover the drawbacks of self-centeredness and the advantages of concern for the welfare of other sentient beings. Because of the practice of cherishing the welfare of other sentient beings, the Buddha achieved omniscience and is now the embodiment of wonderful qualities, whereas we ordinary sentient beings are in a way the embodiment of faults because of our self-centered attitude.

The Buddha first cultivated a mind concerned for the welfare of other sentient beings, then enhanced it, and finally perfected it. This is how he actualized all the wonderful qualities of a Buddha. Therefore, we should realize that here and now we have found this precious human life endowed with excellent qualities, and we are free to engage in spiritual practice. In our spiritual endeavor, the most profound practice is the practice of compassion and the altruistic wish to achieve Buddhahood for the sake of all sentient beings. There is no better practice than this. Therefore, all of us, including the lama, should endeavor to cultivate a compassionate mind in our daily life.

If each of us from the depth of our hearts were to cultivate a mind wishing to benefit other people and other sentient beings, then we would gain a strong sense of confidence, and that would put our minds at ease. When we have that kind of calmness within our minds, even if the whole external environment appears to turn against us and becomes hostile, it will not disturb our mental calm. On the other hand, if our minds are agitated and disturbed and we harbor ill-will toward other sentient beings, even though they have no harmful intentions toward us, our own attitude will make us see everyone as harsh and negative toward us. This reflects our own mental attitude, inner feelings, and experiences. For this reason we will live in constant fear, worry, anxiety, and instability. We may be wealthy and have abundant material facilities at our disposal, but as long as we are disturbed within our minds, we will have no peace. We may be surrounded by our relatives and best friends, but because of our own internal mental attitude, we will have no happiness. Therefore, our inner mental attitude plays a very dominant role. If we have calm and control within our minds, then even if everything around us turns hostile, nothing will disturb us. In fact, for such a person the whole environment is a friend and contributes to his or her mental calm.

Of course, there are many reasons for taking care of ourselves, but we must know how to look after ourselves and pursue our interests in an intelligent way. What we want is happiness, but if in pursuit of our own personal happiness we ignore the welfare of other sentient beings and only bully and deceive them, the results will be negative. If we really want happiness, we must acknowledge that it comes about by taking care of other people. Therefore, we should not forsake the welfare of other sentient beings.

Even if we do not engage in spiritual or religious practice, provided we understand that we have to live interdependently, we will have a peaceful and harmonious life. We are social animals, and we cannot think about living an isolated life with no dependence on other people or other sentient beings. Whatever you do, in all walks of life, whether you are a farmer or a businessman, you have to depend on others. Even within the family you have to depend on the members of your family. This is why people normally live together among families and friends. There are a very few exceptional cases to this, such as the meditating yogis who live in solitude high up in the mountains doing spiritual practices.

Because it is a reality that we are by nature social animals, bound to depend on each other, we need to cultivate affection and concern for other people if we really desire peace and happiness. Look at wild animals and birds. Even they travel together, flock together, and help each other. Bees do not have a particular legal system, they do not follow any spiritual practice, but for their livelihood and survival they depend on each other—that is their natural way of existence. Even though we intelligent human beings must also depend on each other, we sometimes misuse our intelligence and try to exploit each other. That goes against human nature. For those of us who profess to believe in a particular religious practice, it is extremely important that we try to help each other and cultivate a feeling of affection for each other. That is the source of happiness in our life.

The fundamental teaching of Buddha is that we should view others as being more important than we are. Of course, you cannot completely ignore yourself. But neither can you neglect the welfare of other people and other sentient beings, particularly when there is a clash of interest between your own welfare and the welfare of other people. At such a time you should consider other people's welfare as more important than your own personal well being. Compare yourself to the rest of sentient beings. All other sentient beings are countless, while you are just one person. Your suffering and happiness may be very important, but it is just the suffering and happiness of one individual, whereas the happiness and suffering of all other sentient beings is immeasurable and countless. So, it is the way of the wise to sacrifice one for the benefit of the majority and it is the way of the foolish to sacrifice the majority on behalf of just one single individual. Even from the point of view of your personal well being, you must cultivate a compassionate mind—that is the source of happiness in your life.

Irrespective of whether we profess a particular religion or not, we must be warmhearted, we must cultivate compassion, and in that way we will be able to lead peaceful and meaningful lives. In the case of Buddhist practitioners, and particularly Mahayana Buddhist practitioners, how should we engage in the practice? Even when we talk about helping others, we are not talking only about giving them temporary benefit and help, like food, clothing, and shelter and so forth, because these things will not bring long-lasting happiness. Therefore, it is extremely important to investigate the possibility of achieving long-lasting and ultimate happiness. We must judge whether it is possible to eliminate sufferings from their root. Irrespective of whether we are able to practice or not, we should at least cultivate the mental courage that is willing to eliminate sufferings and achieve a state of total cessation of suffering. That will bring strong mental confidence and determination. Therefore, as Mahayana practitioners we should think: "I will help countless mother sentient beings to overcome suffering." That should be our pledge. But if you examine your own present capacity, let alone helping countless sentient beings, you do not have the ability to eliminate the suffering of even one sentient being.

Sufferings arise from specific causes and conditions, which are collected by individual sentient beings. That being so, it is extremely important that individual sentient beings know what is to be practiced and what is to be given up—what brings suffering and what brings long-lasting happiness. We must show sentient beings the right path, which brings happiness and the wrong path, which brings suffering. Therefore, when we talk about benefiting other sentient beings, it is through showing them the path and helping them understand what is to be given up and what is to be practiced. This is how we can help other sentient beings.

In order to do so, it is extremely important, on the one hand, that what you are going to teach to other sentient beings does not remain hidden to you. You must understand the meaning of the path you are going to show other sentient beings. For example, the more advanced a student is in his or her studies, the more that student needs a teacher with better qualifications and greater knowledge. Likewise, in order to show the right path to other sentient beings, you must first have trodden that path yourself. On the other hand, it is not enough that the path you are going to show to other sentient beings is not hidden from you.

You should also know that what you are going to teach other sentient beings is going to help them temporarily and ultimately. Without that knowledge, your teaching may not suit their disposition and interests. It is not enough simply to say that I am doing this with correct motivation. Of course, if you do, there will be no need for regret, but that does not guarantee that it will help other sentient beings. It is for this reason that the scriptures explain the need to actualize different categories of clairvoyance, being able to know the minds and needs of other sentient beings.

Therefore, there are two factors involved here: first, the path and the teaching that you are going to show or give to other sentient beings should not be hidden from you, and secondly you must understand the suitability of such a teaching to the disposition of other sentient beings. You need to understand what dispositions sentient beings have inherited from their past lives. Therefore, unless you become a Buddha yourself and achieve omniscience, your help and guidance may prove to be of only temporary benefit. Cultivating an aspiration to help other sentient beings becomes a cause for cultivating the second wish, wanting to achieve Buddhahood for the sake of all sentient beings. These are the two levels of the awakening mind of bodhichitta.

Such a mind cannot be cultivated in a mere few months or years, but this does not mean it cannot be cultivated at all. If you continue your practice to cultivate bodhichitta, a time will come when you will be successful. For example, in the initial stage you may not even understand the meaning of the word bodhichitta. You might wonder how you could ever cultivate such a mind. But through repeated practice and familiarity, you will gradually come closer to such a mind. It is the nature of conditioned things that they change depending on causes and conditions. So it is important to recall the advantages and benefits of such a mind and cultivate a strong determination to achieve it. Make ardent prayers. Whether you sleep, walk, or sit, you should think: "How good it would be if I could cultivate such a mind." Try to cultivate bodhichitta even on an aspirational level. If you spend your days in such repeated and persistent practice, you can definitely develop it. Make the determination to cultivate it even if it will take many aeons. As Shantideva prays in his *Guide to the Bodhisattva's Way of Life:*

> As long as space endures
> And as long as sentient beings remain,
> May I too abide
> To dispel the sufferings of all sentient beings.

When you engage in a project or an activity that helps other sentient beings, there is no question of a time limit. You must do it continuously. This is how you should train your mind. If you think you will achieve enlightenment or bodhichitta within a few days or months, and if you think that you will get enlightened after entering into a retreat for three years and three months, you are mistaken. When I hear the suggestion that you will attain Buddhahood if you go into retreat for three years and three months, sometimes I jokingly say that this is just like communist propaganda. I tell my Western friends that wanting to practice the most profound and the quickest path is a clear sign that you will achieve no result. How can you achieve the most profound and the vast in the shortest way? The story of the Buddha says that he achieved Buddhahood after three countless aeons. So harboring an expectation to achieve Buddhahood within a short time—like three years and three months—is a clear indication that you will make no real progress. We have to be practical. There is no use in fooling others with your incomplete knowledge.

You should also realize that whether you achieve Buddhahood or not, your purpose is to help other sentient beings. Whether you find yourself in heaven or hell, your purpose is to help other sentient beings. It does not matter how long it takes. You should determine that the altruistic intention to achieve Buddhahood for the sake of all sentient beings will be your only practice, whether you live or die. You must train in cultivating such a mind and understand the aspect and the object of such a mind. Once you gain inferential experience of such a mind, you should receive the Bodhisattva vow, for the vow should be received after you have cultivated a strong wish to engage in the deeds of a Bodhisattva.

What is the Bodhisattva's way of life? It is the way of life that follows naturally from having cultivated the awakening mind of bodhichitta. Omniscience is achieved only through the process of purifying the disturbing emotions within your mind. It cannot be achieved merely through wishes and prayers. We have to train in eliminating all the specific disturbing emotions by relying on specific antidotes. All the activities of a Bodhisattva can be included in two major categories: the practice of skillful means and the practice of wisdom. If the practices of giving, ethics, and so forth are to be perfected, they should be supported and influenced by the practice of wisdom. Without the practice of wisdom, the first five of the six perfections cannot actually become practices of perfection. In order to cultivate such wisdom, you must first cultivate the genuine unmistaken philosophical view that is known as the view of the Middle Way, or Madhyamika.

What is the view of the Madhyamika? There are four schools of philosophical tenets within the Buddhist tradition. Based on an explanation of the first three systems of Buddhist tenets, you can understand the meaning of selflessness on a grosser level, and this will lead finally to the subtle Middle Way view of the selflessness of person and of phenomena, which is contingent on an interpretation of interdependent origination. Having established such an unmistaken correct view and gained conviction in it you will be able to realize emptiness. However, even when you have understood the wisdom realizing emptiness, that alone will not become a powerful antidote to ignorance if it is not supported by other practices such as giving, ethics, patience, and so forth. Mere understanding of selflessness is not sufficient to defeat the disturbing emotions.

Therefore, it is important to cultivate a practice that unites a calmly abiding mind with special insight. In order to develop special insight you must first develop a calmly abiding mind. Calm abiding is single-pointed meditation, whereas special insight refers to discriminative awareness. Through the union of these two, you will be able to engage in a fruitful practice of both method and wisdom.

After generating the conventional awakening mind of bodhichitta, endeavor to cultivate the ultimate awakening mind of bodhichitta. The ultimate bodhichitta is transcendental and free from all elaborations. It is extremely clear, the object of the ultimate, stainless, unwavering, like a butter lamp undisturbed by the wind.

As I explained earlier, conventional bodhichitta refers to the aspirational bodhichitta. What is ultimate bodhichitta? What is transcendental and what is mundane? There are various explanations. All the specific levels of an ordinary being are known as mundane and all the spiritual levels of a superior being, or Arya, are known as transcendental, or supramundane. You achieve the transcendental level when you achieve the path of seeing for the first time. This means that you have realized emptiness directly, although it is possible merely to understand emptiness before achieving the path of seeing.

This text, *Stages of Meditation,* belongs to the Yogachara Svatantrika Madhyamika [Yogic Autonomy Middle Way] school, so when I explain the points made explicitly in the text, I will do so according to the Svatantrika Madhyamika system, but I will elaborate according to the Prasangika Madhyamika [Middle Way Consequentialist] tradition.

There are Aryas, or superior beings, among those practitioners known as Hearers and Solitary Realizers who realize emptiness. But an Arya on the Bodhisattva path realizes emptiness directly because he or she is assisted by the profound practice of method. Such wisdom directly realizing emptiness acts as an opponent to specific disturbing emotions. When we talk about the Four Noble Truths, the true path actually refers to the wisdom realizing emptiness found within the mental continuum of a superior, or Arya, being. This ultimate bodhichitta is also said to be free of all elaborations particularly in the context of the various categories of emptiness, such as the sixteen emptinesses, the twenty emptinesses, the two emptinesses, and so forth.

Although there are as many categories of emptiness as there are types of phenomena, when you realize the emptiness of one specific phenomenon, you also realize the emptiness of all phenomena. The ultimate nature, or emptiness, of all phenomena is of equal taste and of the same undifferentiable nature. Even though the nature of emptiness of all phenomena is the same, and all the different aspects of phenomena, such as whether they are good or bad, or the way they change, arise from the sphere of emptiness, you should understand that emptiness cannot be found apart from the subject or the object.

Emptiness refers to an object's being free of intrinsic existence. Things depend on causes and conditions. This very dependence on causes and conditions signifies that phenomena lack independent, or intrinsic, existence. It also demonstrates how all the diverse aspects of things that we experience arise because they are by nature empty. When we talk about emptiness, we are not dealing with those different aspects, we are dealing with phenomena's ultimate reality. It is from this perspective that the state of emptiness is referred to as free from elaborations. It is also explained that emptiness is uncontaminated, as the verse of homage in Nagarjuna's *Fundamental Wisdom* makes clear:

I pay homage to that being sublime
Amongst the Buddhas, the propounder of the teaching,
Who taught that things arise through dependence
And that there is no cessation, no birth,
No annihilation, no permanence,
No coming and no going,
No separate meaning and no sameness,
Thoroughly free from elaborations, and completely at peace.

Emptiness and dependent arising are two sides of the same coin. From the perspective of dependent arising, or the conventional perspective, things arise, things can be produced, and things cease. The verse I have quoted from *Fundamental Wisdom* means that things are not produced, do not cease, are not annihilated, nor are they permanent in any independent way. In terms of time there is also neither any independent annihilation nor permanence. From the point of view of the object there is no independent going and coming. Nagarjuna described eight categories of elaboration, for example production and cessation and how they do not occur independently. It is said that the Aryas, or superior beings, whose direct perception of wisdom is uncontaminated, have not seen the independent existence of the production or cessation of dependently arising phenomenon. Their minds see only the ultimate truth, emptiness, which is free of all elaborations.

Ultimate reality, or ultimate bodhichitta, is described as extremely clear. It is referred to as "ultimate," because it is the object of engagement of an ultimate wisdom. It is also called stainless and unwavering. In other words, the wisdom of a superior being in meditative absorption is a wisdom that is a combination of a calmly abiding mind and special insight. Such a combination is achieved by first cultivating calm abiding. Once you gain stability with regard to the object of investigation, you can focus your understanding upon it without being disturbed by the mental laxity and excitement of conceptual thoughts. Such wisdom is referred to as unwavering and is compared to a butter lamp undisturbed by the breeze.

This ultimate bodhichitta is transcendental and free from all elaborations. The way to achieve this is explained in the following lines:

> **This is achieved through constant and respectful familiarity with the yoga of calm abiding meditation and special insight over a long period of time. The *Unraveling of the Thought Sutra* says, "O Maitreya, you must know that all the virtuous Dharmas of Hearers, Bodhisattvas, or Tathagatas, whether worldly or transcendental, are the fruits of calm abiding meditation and special insight." Since all kinds of concentrations can be included in these two, all yogis must at all times seek calm abiding meditation and special insight. Again the *Unraveling of the Thought Sutra* says, "The Buddha has said it must be known that the teachings of various types of concentrations sought by his Hearers, Bodhisattvas, and Tathagatas are all contained in calm abiding meditation and special insight."**

A calmly abiding mind refers to a state of mind in which your mind abides on the object of your choice and in which the mind is not distracted to external objects other than the object of your mental focus and meditation. Your mind remains stable, focused on the object, and free from laxity and excitement. Such a mind is also referred to as a single-pointed concentration, and through its stability you are able to achieve mental bliss. Special insight refers to gaining special insight into the ultimate reality of the object on which your mind is focused. There are two categories of special insight: mundane and transcendental. There could be different objects according to different categories of special insight, but here special insight refers to the mind that focuses on emptiness.

Buddha Shakyamuni taught these two practices, calm abiding and special insight, and they are the only methods by which you can achieve all the levels of concentration. Therefore, the text states that since calm abiding and special insight are equally important, you should cultivate both qualities:

> **Yogis cannot eliminate mental obscurations merely by familiarizing themselves with calm abiding meditation alone. It will only suppress the disturbing emotions and delusions temporarily. Without the light of wisdom, the latent potential of the disturbing emotions cannot be thoroughly destroyed, and therefore their complete destruction will not be possible. For this reason the *Unraveling of the Thought Sutra* says, "Concentration can suppress the disturbing emotions properly, and wisdom can thoroughly destroy their latent potential."**

Merely meditating on calm abiding will not enable you to eliminate obscurations to enlightenment and the disturbing emotions. Even if you achieve calm abiding meditation with reference to emptiness, that alone is not enough to remove the obscurations if it is not supported by the practice of special insight.

The *Unraveling of the Thought Sutra* also says,

> **Even if you meditate with single-pointed concentration**
> **You will not destroy the misconception of the self**
> **And your disturbing emotions will disturb you again;**
> **This is like Udrak's single-pointed meditation.**

Calm abiding meditation alone will not be able to remove the afflictive emotions and destroy the misconception of self. Disturbing emotions will arise again and disturb you once more, as happened in the case of the non-Buddhist master called Udrak. He meditated on calm abiding for a long time, in the course of which his hair grew very long. While he was completely absorbed in single-pointed concentration, some of his hair was eaten by rats. As soon as he rose from his meditation and saw that rats had eaten his hair, he became angry and thus his disturbing emotions came back again. Although the disturbing emotions did not arise while he was absorbed in single-pointed meditation, that they returned after he rose from his meditation clearly shows that calm abiding meditation alone does not put an end to the disturbing emotions.

> **When the selflessness of phenomena is examined specifically,**
> **And meditations are performed on the basis of that analysis,**
> **That is the cause of the resultant liberation;**
> **No other cause can bring peace.**

So, specifically examining the selflessness of phenomena means that by employing special insight, or discriminative awareness, we can be liberated. We cannot employ any other technique to achieve liberation, or nirvana.

> **Also the *Bodhisattva Section* says, "Those who haven't heard these various teachings of the Bodhisattva Collection and have also not heard the implemented teaching on Monastic Discipline, who think that single-pointed concentration alone is enough, will fall into the pit of arrogance due to pride. As such, they cannot gain complete release from rebirth, old age, sickness, death, misery, lamentation, suffering, mental unhappiness, and disturbances. Neither do they gain complete liberation from the cycle of the six states of existence, nor from the heaps of suffering mental and physical aggregates. Keeping this in mind, the Tathagata has said that hearing the teachings will help you gain liberation from old age and death."**

So, you should listen to explanations of the meaning of suchness and then meditate on it, and that will help you to achieve liberation from suffering.

> **For these reasons, those who wish to attain the thoroughly purified transcendent wisdom by eliminating all obscurations should meditate on wisdom while remaining in calm abiding meditation.**

Chapter 6

Wisdom

According to Buddhist tradition, the validity of a philosophical doctrine is determined by logical reasoning. The Buddha very clearly stated:

> Bhikshus and scholars should examine my words
> In the way that a goldsmith tests gold by burning,
> cutting, and rubbing.
> Only then should my words be accepted,
> Not out of respect for me.

Therefore, in the process of establishing both external and internal phenomena, we must rely on reasoning. There is no need to rely on scriptural authority alone. What is taught in scriptural texts can be analyzed in the light of reason, and the validity of their contents can be established. The Buddha's own words are open to examination. One of the most wonderful features of Buddhist culture is that the practitioner has the right to examine the teachings. The words of the teacher can also be examined.

The Buddhist approach to knowledge is similar to that of modern science. Initially you should not make any definitive statement on a subject of contention, but examine the issue impartially. The result should be determined through analysis, examining the evidence with reason. In general, Buddhism has a high regard for logical reasoning.

It is important to establish the basis, path, and result. Basis here refers to the fact, or reality, of phenomena. We follow a spiritual path based on that fact and so achieve a result. Spiritual practice is not a mere fabrication of the mind, but something that really exists. If the basis of spiritual practice were a mere figment of the imagination, it would not have the potential to change and transform our minds through the practice of the path. Consequently, liberation and so forth could not be explained as a result.

The resultant state of a Buddha is endowed with many great qualities. These qualities are produced by cultivating the appropriate causes and conditions and by engaging in the practice of the spiritual path. The ten powers and other attributes of a Buddha are developed in due course because individuals have the potential to produce such qualities. Generally speaking, nothing can be produced without a base, or a foundation. It would be absurd to assert that omniscience is produced from rocks and mountains. It is much more logical to say that engaging in the combined path of skillful means and wisdom on the basis of consciousness can produce omniscience.

Establishing the base is a very crucial step. It distinguishes what exists from mere mental fabrication. It refers to proper identification of the laws of nature and reality. Therefore, in order to establish the true nature of the base, it is important to be objective.

There are various interpretations of Buddha's scriptural teachings by his followers. When a scriptural teaching cannot stand logical analysis, its meaning is interpreted within the context of three criteria: intention, purpose, and contradiction. For instance, if a sutra deals with ultimate reality but under analysis the apparent meaning is found to be faulty, it is interpreted according to the intention and purpose for which it was taught. Similarly, when those aspects of selflessness that are obscure are found to be faulty through examination by inferential logic, there is no need to accept them. These days, the sun and the moon, along with their size, their distance from the earth, and their movements, have become more obvious to us. So if a scriptural text describes such obvious things in ways that contradict our direct valid perception, we no longer accept them as true. In general, Buddhism and science take a similar approach to such things.

Buddhist teachings are presented within the context of the spiritual base, path, and fruit. The fruit concerns the many great qualities the practitioner manifests when he or she attains Buddhahood. In order to achieve such qualities, you need to produce the right causes and conditions. This process consists of an integrated spiritual practice. It is important to know that each one of us has the potential to develop the ten powers and other wonderful qualities of a Buddha. This potential is innate within the continuity of our consciousness. Generally speaking, nothing can be produced without an appropriate basis or foundation. Just as it would be absurd to state that rocks and mountains can attain omniscience by way of spiritual practice, it is clear that those who possess consciousness can attain omniscience.

The spiritual basis in this case refers to the intrinsic nature of the mind that has the potential to awaken to the state of full enlightenment. The spiritual path consists of aspects of method and wisdom, which means that a practitioner accumulates merit and insight and so transcends to Buddhahood. Its is essential to understand these fundamentals of Buddhist philosophy. They are not figments of someone's imagination, but conform to reality. If they were mere imaginary things, no matter how much effort you put in, you would make no progress on the path. You would gain no result and you would not be able to explain how to attain liberation. You should be open-minded and impartial in examining these fundamental principles. If you have preconceived ideas influenced by other philosophical views, you will find it hard to appreciate these principles objectively.

We should examine and analyze questions and accept those findings that are logical. There may be matters for which Buddhist tradition has an explanation that science has not yet discovered, and so has nothing to say about them. But when we are dealing with scientifically proven facts, we should not be dogmatic about what is stated in our texts. As I said earlier, this text primarily deals with the two truths as the basis, the practice of method and wisdom as the spiritual path, and the attainments of the wisdom and the physical body of an enlightened being as the result.

Those who wish to attain that transcendent wisdom that is totally free of all obscurations should meditate on wisdom while abiding in single-pointed concentration.

> **The *Heap of Jewels Sutra* says: "Single-pointed concentration is achieved by adhering to moral ethics. With the achievement of single-pointed concentration, you meditate on wisdom. Wisdom helps you to attain a pure pristine awareness. Through pure pristine awareness your moral conduct is perfected."**

In order to accomplish the purposes of both others and ourselves, all obscurations should be eliminated. Those who intend to realize transcendent wisdom in such a way should initially practice calm abiding meditation. A practitioner who has the ability to analyze phenomena with the wisdom realizing suchness while engaging in calm abiding meditation can generate special insight.

In terms of practice, the three trainings are presented in a definite sequence. Let me elaborate. The text reads, "Wisdom helps you to attain a pure pristine awareness." A perfectly transcendent wisdom has the ability to eradicate the obscurations along with their seeds. Wisdom realizing conventional truth, however powerful, does not have that ability. Therefore we can conclude that to do so, it must be a wisdom realizing the ultimate truth. In this context, perfectly transcendental wisdom refers to omniscience. And in order to attain omniscience, obscurations to liberation, or disturbing emotions, and obscurations to knowledge, must be eliminated. Wisdom alone is the direct opponent that enables us to eradicate the two obscurations and their seeds or latent potencies. Neither ethical discipline nor single-pointed concentration can confront them directly. Wisdom here refers to the wisdom derived from meditation, not that derived from listening and contemplation. Therefore, to actualize that special insight realizing ultimate reality, you must first become proficient in calm abiding meditation. Since this single-pointed concentration is a positive thought, subtle mental dullness and excitement must be abandoned. In order to abandon these faults, you must first train in practices of ethical discipline.

The *Meditation on Faith in the Mahayana Sutra* says: "O child of noble family, if you do not abide by wisdom, I cannot say how you will have faith in the Mahayana of the Bodhisattvas, or how you will set forth in the Mahayana."

This concerns generation of faith, or the conviction that comes with knowledge. Unless the "child of noble family," or a practitioner, is able to develop the wisdom of special insight, generation of faith based on knowledge is not possible. Of course, a person can have devoted faith, but when he or she develops faith as a result of comprehending ultimate reality, it is supported by reason and knowledge. For instance, true renunciation can be developed when the system of liberation is properly understood. The individual gains certainty that, in general, liberation is possible and is something that can be developed within our stream of consciousness. Such a sense of renunciation definitely has distinctive qualities. Similarly, the strength of our taking refuge improves as we refine our knowledge of emptiness.

"O child of noble family, you should know that this is because Bodhisattvas' faith in the Mahayana and setting forth in the Mahayana occurs as a result of contemplating the perfect Dharma and reality with a mind free of distraction."

This clearly indicates the need to develop a wisdom examining conventional and ultimate reality single-pointedly in order to enable the practitioner to gain firm conviction and faith in the spiritual basis, path, and result that are taught in the Mahayana system.

> **A yogi's mind will be distracted to various objects if he cultivates only special insight without developing a calmly abiding mind. It will be unstable, like a butter lamp in wind. Since clarity of pristine awareness will be absent, these two [special insight and a calmly abiding mind] should be cultivated equally. Therefore, the *Sutra of the Great and Complete Transcendence of Suffering* says: "Hearers cannot see Buddha-nature because their single-pointed absorption is stronger and wisdom is weaker."**

If this is interpreted in terms of the philosophical systems that assert that followers of the paths of Hearers and Solitary Realizers do not realize the selflessness, or emptiness, of phenomena it is said that they do not see Buddha-nature with a wisdom analyzing reality. They only realize the selflessness of persons, not the selflessness of phenomena. This is because their concentration is more powerful than their wisdom. If this is interpreted in terms of the Aryas, or exalted beings, among the Hearers and Solitary Realizers, who are like Mahayana Aryas in realizing emptiness, then the assertion that Hearers are not able to see Buddha-nature means that their realization of the nature of the contaminated mind is not based on the application of a wide variety of logic and reasoning. This is because their single-pointed concentration is strong and their wisdom is weak.

"Bodhisattvas can see it, but not clearly, because their wisdom is stronger and their single-pointed concentration is weaker. Whereas Tathagatas can see all, because they possess a calmly abiding mind and special insight to an equal degree."

This point is difficult, isn't it? But we can provide a couple of interpretations. Firstly, I think that the author meant to say here that even though Bodhisattvas have direct apprehension of suchness, they apprehend suchness directly only during meditative absorption, not during the post-meditation period. However, for Buddhas, realization of suchness is total and complete. Therefore, they have direct apprehension of suchness at all times regardless of whether they are meditating or not.

Secondly, this verse could mean that even though Bodhisattvas directly apprehend the suchness of the mind, they do not apprehend it clearly. This is due to the latent potency of mental defilements, which they have yet to eliminate. On the other hand, Buddhas are completely and thoroughly free of the slightest defilement and have eliminated their latent potential entirely. Their knowledge of suchness is excellent.

Due to the power of calm abiding meditation, the mind will not be disturbed by the wind of conceptual thoughts, like a butter lamp undisturbed by the breeze. Special insight eliminates every stain of wrong views, thus you will not be affected by [the views of] others. The *Moon Lamp Sutra* says: "By the force of calm abiding meditation, the mind will become unwavering, and with special insight it will become like a mountain." Therefore, maintain a yogic practice of them both.

This indicates the characteristic, or meaning, of calm abiding meditation and penetrative insight. Calm abiding is a quality of the mind that single-pointedly attends to its object, free of all external and internal distractions. The mind does not focus on any object except the object of its concentration. Since it is free of any mental dullness, the object is apprehended with utmost clarity. Prolonged development of such a single-pointed mind results in the bliss of physical and mental pliancy. And when such a single-pointed concentration is conjoined with bliss, it is characterized as calm abiding meditation. Special insight is a wisdom realizing emptiness conjoined with physical and mental bliss. This bliss is derived from the analytical wisdom, which examines the reality of its object over and over again, based on the bliss of calm abiding meditation. This insight does not remain satisfied with the mere placement of the mind on its object. Whatever the object, whether it concerns conventional or ultimate reality, it is thoroughly examined by analytical wisdom.

Chapter 7

Common Prerequisites for Meditating on Calm Abiding and Special Insight

How should calm abiding meditation and special insight be practiced together?

> **Initially the yogi should seek the prerequisites that can assist him in actualizing calm abiding meditation and special insight quickly and easily.**

It is clear that practitioners need to rely on these prerequisites in order to gain spiritual realizations.

> **The prerequisites necessary for the development of calm abiding meditation are: to live in a conducive environment, to limit your desires and practice contentment, not being involved in too many activities, maintaining pure moral ethics, and fully eliminating attachment and all other kinds of conceptual thoughts.**

Kamalashila next explains what a conducive, or favorable, environment means.

> A conducive environment should be known by these five characteristics: providing easy access to food and clothes, being free of evil beings and enemies, being free from disease, containing good friends who maintain moral ethics and who share similar views, and being visited by few people in the daytime and with little noise at night.
>
> Limiting your desires refers to not being excessively attached to many or good clothes, such as religious robes, and so forth. The practice of contentment means always being satisfied with any little thing, like inferior religious robes, and so forth. Not being involved in many activities refers to giving up ordinary activities like business, avoiding too close association with householders and monks, and totally abandoning the practice of medicine and astrology.

Association in this context refers to gathering and gossiping on and on without any purpose. For those who are able to meditate with much concentration, the practices of medicine and astrology become impediments. Therefore, unless there are special reasons to do otherwise, practitioners are instructed to avoid these worldly pursuits.

> Even in the case of the statement that a transgression of the Hearers' vows cannot be restored, if there is regret and an awareness of the intention not to repeat it, and an awareness of the lack of a true identity of the mind that performed the action, or familiarity with the lack of a true identity of all phenomena, that person's morality can be said to be pure. This should be understood from the *Sutra on the Elimination of*

> ***Ajatashatru's Regret.*** **You should overcome your regret and make special effort in meditation.**

The two types of moral ethics refer to the vows of individual liberation and the Bodhisattva's vow. It could also mean the vows of ordained people and the vows of lay people.

The following passage deals with the futility of desire and the need to distance yourself from mundane activities. To this end it is important to discard all types of misconceptions.

> **Being mindful of the various defects of attachment in this life and future lives helps eliminate misconceptions in this regard. Some common features of both beautiful and ugly things in the cycle of existence are that they are all unstable and subject to disintegration. It is beyond doubt that you will be separated from all of these things without delay. So, meditate on why you should be so excessively attached to these things and then discard all misconceptions.**
>
> **What are the prerequisites of special insight? They are relying on holy persons, seriously seeking extensive instruction, and proper contemplation.**

In this context, contemplation concerns meditation on both conventional and ultimate realities. Now the text explains the characteristics of a spiritual guide.

> **What type of holy person should you rely upon? One who has heard many [teachings], who expresses himself clearly, who is endowed with compassion, and able to withstand hardship.**

Clear expression means skillful speech, but without compassion it does not go very far. When compassion is missing, even great learning is of little use. For a teacher to be productive and effective in the process of teaching, compassion, or a kind heart, is explained here as the most crucial quality. There are other defects in teaching, for example being tired of explaining to the students. So being tolerant and patient in the face of such difficulties is also important.

> **What is meant by seriously seeking extensive instruction? This is to listen seriously with respect to the definitive and interpretable meaning of the twelve branches of the Buddha's teachings. The *Unraveling of the Thought Sutra* says: "Not listening to superior beings' teachings as you wish is an obstacle to special insight." The same sutra says, "Special insight arises from its cause, correct view, which in turn arises from listening and contemplation." *The Questions of Narayana Sutra* says, "Through the experience of listening [to teachings] you gain wisdom, and with wisdom disturbing emotions are thoroughly pacified."**

The above passage very clearly and succinctly explains the advantages of acquiring a vast knowledge by way of listening and contemplation. This specifically refers to the value of a rich and versatile knowledge of the scriptural teachings.

> **What is meant by proper contemplation? It is properly establishing the definitive and interpretable sutras. When Bodhisattvas are free of doubt, they can**

meditate single-pointedly. Otherwise, if doubt and indecision beset them, they will be like a man at a crossroads uncertain of which path to follow.

Whatever you have heard, it is extremely important to ascertain its meaning by means of contemplation. Otherwise, you will be like an indecisive person at a crossroads. Indecision and doubt naturally impede your proficiency in teaching and explaining the subject to students.

In the above passage, the text refers to definitive and interpretable sutras. What is meant by definitive and interpretable teachings? What are the definitive and interpretable sutras? This is one of the crucial concerns of Buddhist philosophy. Popularly, the Buddha is said to have given three rounds of teachings, which are known as the three Turnings of the Wheel of Dharma. The first round presented the Four Noble Truths. The exposition of the Four Noble Truths formed the framework and foundation of Buddhism. The four truths are the truth of suffering, the truth of the origin of suffering, true paths, and true cessations.

In the second Turning of the Wheel of Dharma, the Buddha dealt exclusively and exhaustively with the Noble Truth of cessation. There are indications that the perfection of wisdom scriptures originated from this teaching. Since there were individuals who could not comprehend the notion of selflessness as taught during the second Turning of the Wheel, and since it was possible that some people might develop wrong views in relation to this teaching, during the third Turning of the Wheel, the discourse on selflessness was clarified in the context of three different phenomena: imputed phenomena, dependent phenomena, and thoroughly established phenomena. Imputed phenomena are said to be selfless because they do not have an intrinsic identity. Dependent phenomena are said to be selfless because they lack the identity of being self-produced, and the thoroughly established phenomena are said to be selfless because they lack any ultimate identity.

However, certain sutras taught during the third Turning of the Wheel, such as the *Tathagata Essence Sutra*, explained the clear light of the subjective mind in addition to the clear light of the object, or the emptiness that had been flawlessly explained during the second Turning of the Wheel. The nature of mind was dealt with in greater detail. Since the fourth Noble Truth, the truth of the path, was more explicitly and profoundly expounded, this naturally established a link to understanding the teachings on tantra.

The Buddha gave his teachings with the sole purpose of benefiting those who listened to them. He employed skillful means to achieve this goal, giving teachings on the greater and lesser vehicles in the context of people's greater or lesser mental scope. The various philosophical tenets were taught to suit varying degrees of intelligence. Consequently, there are four Buddhist schools of thought. Broadly speaking, some schools contend that during the first sermon the Buddha taught only the sixteen attributes of the Four Noble Truths. They assert that there were no teachings on emptiness, but only on the selflessness of persons.

Some of the scriptures containing the Buddha's teachings cannot be accepted literally. This is why we need to categorize them as definitive and interpretable teachings. The definitions of these terms also vary according to different schools of thought. The Chittamatra School defines definitive teachings as those whose meaning can be accepted literally, and interpretable teachings as those whose meaning cannot be accepted literally. The Svatantrika Madhyamika School defines definitive scriptures as those teachings which have ultimate truth as their direct and principal topic of discussion, and which can be accepted literally. Teachings of the Buddha other than these belong among the interpretable scriptures.

In order to ascertain the ultimate truth, subtle emptiness, we must follow the sutras and commentaries that flawlessly expound the subject. To this end we must understand the scriptural texts in their proper sequence and according to whether they are definitive or require interpretation. This may not initially be very simple. But, if we follow the great beings who have pointed out which scriptures are definitive and which interpretable, and search for emptiness by studying these sutras and the commentaries to them, we will be able to realize the view of emptiness. Thus, Kamalashila stresses the importance of studying both definitive and interpretable sutras.

The text here deals with the common prerequisites of calm abiding meditation and special insight.

> **Yogis should at all times avoid fish, meat, and so forth, should eat with moderation, and avoid foods that are not conducive to health.**

Meditators need to be physically healthy. Therefore, proper

diet is essential. On the other hand, their minds should be clear and strong and this will also contribute to physical health. For these reasons, it is recommended that they give up eating fish, meat, garlic, onions, etc. Appropriate food should be eaten in moderation, for indigestion can cause havoc with meditation. What's more, those who overeat can hardly stay awake.

> **Thus, Bodhisattvas who have assembled all the prerequisites for calm abiding meditation and special insight should enter into meditation.**

There are other practices such as not sleeping during the first and the last periods of the night. While sleeping during the middle part of the night, cultivate mindfulness and maintain a proper posture.

If a vegetarian diet does not result in protein deficiency, it is a wholesome way of living. Even if you cannot be a strict vegetarian, at least moderating the amount of meat you eat is beneficial. Within the southern schools of Buddhism eating meat is not strictly prohibited, but the meat of certain animals, such as those that are not cloven-hoofed or those that have been slaughtered specifically for your consumption, is forbidden. This means that meat bought casually in the market is acceptable.

Such meat that may be eaten is referred to as "pure meat" and is distinguished by three qualifications: that you have not seen the animal being killed for you to eat, that you have not received any information in this connection, and that you have no doubt that the animal has not been killed for your consumption. In general, Mahayana Buddhist schools also do not prohibit the eating of meat. However, certain scriptures, such as the *Descent into Lanka Sutra,* strictly prohibit eating meat at all times, whereas other scriptures, like the *Essence of Madhyamaka* by Acharya Bhavaviveka, seem to permit it. Thus, some Mahayana texts concerning the perfection of wisdom prohibit eating meat, while others do not. The three lower classes of tantra strictly prohibit the eating of meat, whereas the highest class permits it. Certain ritual practices within this class of tantra require the five kinds of meat and five kinds of nectar. The general standard, therefore, is that meat openly available in the market may be eaten, but we are prohibited from killing animals for our own consumption.

As explained earlier, interested practitioners who enjoy the necessary facilities and freedom from interference should fulfill the preparatory practices before beginning calm abiding meditation.

> **When meditating, the yogi should first complete all the preparatory practices. He should go to the toilet and in a pleasant location free of disturbing noise he should think, "I will deliver all sentient beings to the state of enlightenment." Then he should manifest great compassion, the thought wishing to liberate all sentient beings, and pay homage to all the Buddhas and Bodhisattvas in the ten directions by touching the five limbs of his body to the ground.**

Invoke a merit-field by visualizing Buddhas and Bodhisattvas in the space in front of you and make prayers. This is an exclusively sutric practice. When the invocation is done in relation to tantra, you generate the commitment being and merge the wisdom being with it. When you make prostrations, tradition recommends that you do so by touching your five limbs—your forehead, two palms, and two knees—to the ground. The important thing is that it should be done properly and with delight. It is unwholesome to perform prostrations either as a mere formality or under coercion.

Representations of the Buddha's Body, Speech, and Mind can be arranged physically on an altar or can be visualized in the space in front of you. Offerings should be made according to your means. If you are fortunate and wealthy, well and good. But if you do not have the means to obtain many images of the Buddha, there is no need to acquire them improperly. Statues and thangkas acquired by fraud and deceit, instead of bringing virtue, bring only negative consequences.

If you are a solitary monk in retreat in the mountains, too many religious images will only tempt thieves to no great purpose. In the past, great saints like Milarepa possessed high realizations but no such images. Milarepa lived in an empty cave. There is a story that one night a thief entered his cave, searching for something to steal. Mila laughed and asked him, "What are you looking for? When I cannot find anything in the daytime, what do you expect to find at night?" Thus, we should remember that spiritual realizations are developed within, and that external objects are not of much consequence.

There are people who in the name of religious practice struggle hard to erect an elaborate and costly altar. Loaded with images it becomes part of their household furniture and ceases to be of much significance or purpose. So, if you can obtain representations of the Buddha's Body, Speech, and Mind in an acceptable manner, you should have a statue of Shakyamuni Buddha, the founder of Buddhism. To represent his speech, you can set up a copy of the *Perfection of Wisdom Sutra* as the main text together with a copy of the *Avatamsaka Sutra,* which deals with the deeds of Bodhisattvas. Next to them you can place those things which represent the mind of the Buddhas.

If you cannot obtain these things, don't worry about it. But if you can, they should be arranged in a proper way. In the center should be a painting, statue, or similar image of Buddha Shakyamuni. Around him should be representations of meditational deities in both peaceful and wrathful aspects, and representations of the Buddha's eight great immediate disciples. If, on the other hand, these images are arranged according to their monetary value, the quality of the material from which they are made, or whether they are new or antique, then you are making a serious mistake. To do so would reveal that you viewed these holy images as nothing more than material possessions.

So, with understanding of its meaning and purpose, arrange your altar in the proper order. Make prostrations and arrange offerings before the holy objects. You should be careful about what you offer. If you offer what are called "pure materials," you can accumulate immense virtue. Conversely, if the materials are "impure," then instead of gaining virtue you are liable to face negative consequences. "Impure materials" refers to things acquired by the five wrong livelihoods, such as flattery, deceit, and so forth. This is of particular concern for ordained people.

When people treat scriptures and statues or photos of Buddhas as commercial items and do business with them for personal gain, it is wrong livelihood. It is certainly unwholesome and has serious negative consequences. On the other hand, when people work to publish scriptural texts, make statues, and so forth, in order to propagate the Buddha's doctrine, it is a different matter. In such cases, when individuals are motivated to help those in need of such religious support, they are engaged in wholesome activities. We must, therefore, realize the importance of offering pure materials. There is a widespread tradition among Tibetans of offering bowls of water and butter lamps. This, too, should be done respectfully and in a proper manner.

The practice of making offerings is followed by confession, rejoicing, requesting teachings, beseeching the Buddhas not to enter parinirvana, and dedication. Together, these steps are known as the seven-branch practice. Highly realized beings engage in such valuable practices in their quest to accumulate vast merit.

> **He should place an image of the Buddhas and Bodhisattvas, such as a painting, in front of him or in some other place. He should make as many offerings and praises as he can. He should confess his misdeeds and rejoice in the merit of all other beings.**

The meditator should first perform the seven-branch practices such as prostration, offering, requesting the teachings, and so forth.

> **Then, he should sit in the full lotus posture of Vairochana, or the half lotus posture, on a comfortable cushion. The eyes should not be too widely opened or too tightly closed. Let them focus on the tip of the nose. The body should not be bent forward or backward. Keep it straight and turn the attention inwards. The shoulders should rest in their natural position and the head should not lean back, forward, or to either side. The nose should be in line with the navel. The teeth**

> **and lips should rest in their natural state with the tongue touching the upper palate. Breathe very gently and softly without causing any noise, without laboring, and without unevenness. Inhale and exhale naturally, slowly, and unnoticeably.**

Meditators need to pay special attention to the way they breathe. Breathing should be free of any noise or congestion. Violent breathing is harmful. Breathe gently and deeply. Inhale and exhale calmly and evenly.

Chapter 8

The Practice of Calm Abiding

Calm abiding meditation should be achieved first. Calm abiding is that mind which has overcome distraction to external objects, and which spontaneously and continuously turns toward the object of meditation with bliss and pliancy.

After properly fulfilling the preparatory practices, you should engage in the actual meditation, which consists of calm abiding and special insight. What is this calm abiding meditation? It is that state of mind that naturally attends to the object of meditation as a result of pacifying distraction to external objects.

Besides that, it gradually eliminates the defects of the body and mind due to its being free from mental dullness and excitement. "With bliss and pliancy" refers to these physical and mental qualities that a meditator develops. In the process of meditation, mental pliancy is developed first and is followed by physical pliancy. Interestingly, physical bliss is generated after that, followed by mental bliss. When the mind is conjoined with bliss, it is known as calm abiding meditation.

What is special insight?

> **That which properly examines suchness from within a state of calm abiding is special insight. The *Cloud of Jewels Sutra* reads, "Calm abiding meditation is a single-pointed mind; special insight makes specific analysis of the ultimate."**

After developing the ability to engage in calm abiding meditation, the meditator does not single-pointedly place the mind on the object, but starts examining it. The object of meditation here is primarily ultimate truth, but conventional phenomena are not excluded. The concentration that generates physical and mental bliss by the force of analyzing the object is special insight. Thereafter, a union of calm abiding and special insight is attained.

Calm abiding and special insight are not differentiated according to their objects of concentration. They can both take conventional and ultimate truth as objects. There is calm abiding meditation that focuses on the ultimate truth, and there is special insight that meditates on conventional truth. For instance, there is calm abiding meditation in which the mind is single-pointedly placed on emptiness. Special insight also meditates on conventional phenomena such as the subtle and grosser aspects of the meditative paths.

In general, the difference between these two types of meditation is that calm abiding is a concentrative meditation and special insight an analytical one. The Perfection Vehicle and the first three classes of tantra share this notion. According to the highest tantra, special insight is a concentrative meditation. This is a unique mode of understanding within the context of which special insight operates fully as a concentrative meditation. On the other hand, the Great Seal of Mahamudra of the Kagyu tradition and the Great Accomplishment, or Dzogchen, of the Nyingma tradition deal only with analytical meditation.

> **Also, from the *Unraveling of the Thought Sutra:* "Maitreya asked, 'O Buddha, how should [people] thoroughly search for calm abiding meditation and gain expertise in special insight?' The Buddha answered, 'Maitreya, I have given the following teachings to Bodhisattvas: sutras, melodious praises, prophetic teachings, verses, specific instructions, advice from specific experiences, expressions of realization, legends, birth tales, extensive teachings, established doctrine, and instructions.**
>
> **'Bodhisattvas should properly listen to these teachings, remember their contents, train in verbal recitation, and thoroughly examine them mentally. With perfect comprehension, they should go alone to remote areas and reflect on these teachings and continue to focus their minds upon them. They should focus mentally only on those topics that they have reflected about and maintain this continuously. That is called mental engagement.'"**

In calm abiding meditation, you single-pointedly focus the mind on the essential and summary points of the teaching. The Buddha's teachings, as described in these twelve categories, are extensive and cover vast topics such as those concerning the mental and physical aggregates, elements, sources of perception, and so forth. In the context of calm abiding meditation, you are not to elaborate, but are to attend to the essential nature or the point of the teaching, whether it be emptiness or impermanence, and contemplate its nature. On the other hand, meditation on special insight is analytical. The meditator elaborates on the identity, origin, and other characteristics of the objects of meditation, such as the aggregates, elements, sources of perception, and so forth.

> **"'When the mind has been repeatedly engaged in this way and physical and mental pliancy have been achieved, that mind is called calm abiding. This is how Bodhisattvas properly seek the calmly abiding mind.'"**

Through the process of meditation, the practitioner initially actualizes mental pliancy. This is preceded by a kind of heaviness of the brain that is in fact a sign of relinquishing the defects of the mind. After generating mental pliancy, physical pliancy is actualized. This is the direct opponent of the physical defects. Physical bliss is generated as a result, and from this mental bliss is generated.

> **"'When the Bodhisattva has achieved physical and mental pliancy and abides only in them, he eliminates mental distraction. The phenomenon that has been contemplated as the object of inner single-pointed concentration should be analyzed and regarded as like a reflection. This reflection or image, which is the object of single-pointed concentration, should be thoroughly**

discerned as an object of knowledge. It should be completely investigated and thoroughly examined. Practice patience and take delight in it. With proper analysis, observe and understand it. This is what is known as special insight. Thus, Bodhisattvas are skilled in the ways of special insight.'"

Generation of a positive motivation is crucial. The practitioner should recreate this positive attitude throughout the process of practice. Think, "I shall listen to this holy text by the great Kamalashila in order to attain unsurpassed Buddhahood for the sake of all sentient beings as vast as space." It is highly important that we realize the rarity and preciousness of the human life. It is on this basis that we can attain both temporary and ultimate goals. This life as a free and fortunate human being is a great occasion and we should take full advantage of it. The root and foundation for realizing the ultimate goal of enlightenment is generation of the altruistic thought, and this in turn derives from compassion. Other complementary practices essential in this context are the practice of generosity and other meritorious deeds, and training in concentration, which is the union of calm abiding and special insight.

Before generating compassion for other sentient beings, the practitioner must think about the sufferings of cyclic existence in general, and in particular the sufferings of the different realms within the cycle of existence. Through this process of contemplation, the practitioner comes to appreciate the unbearable nature of the miseries of the cycle of existence. This naturally leads you to find out how to abandon them. Is there an occasion when we can be completely free of suffering? What methods need to be applied in order to relinquish suffering? When you earnestly engage in such an inquiry and examine the question well, you will realize what causes sufferings. The source of suffering is the mental defilement that arises from action and disturbing emotions. This is temporary and the mind can be completely separated from it. The practitioner comes to realize that the Noble Truth of cessation can be attained with the pacification, or elimination, of suffering and its causes. The corollary is that the individual develops renunciation, wishing for freedom from suffering and its causes. And when you wish for other sentient beings also to gain freedom from suffering and its causes, you are taking a major step toward generating compassion.

First a practitioner should train in the stages of the common path and then gradually incorporate the stages of the greater path. This is a sound and correct mode of actualizing a spiritual career.

After having performed the preparatory practices, you undertake the training in the two types of awakening mind. These two are the conventional and ultimate awakening minds. With generation of the conventional awakening mind, a practitioner engages in the deeds of a Bodhisattva, which include the six perfections. Meditation on the ultimate awakening mind is done by generating a transcendental wisdom directly realizing emptiness. Such a wisdom is a meditative stabilization that is a union of calm abiding and special insight. This means that while focussing single-pointedly you can simultaneously analyze the nature of emptiness.

First the practitioner must gather the prerequisites and other conditions conducive to meditation on calm abiding.

> **The yogis who are interested in actualizing a calmly abiding mind should initially concentrate closely on the fact that the twelve sets of scriptures—the sutras, melodious praises, and so forth—can be summarized as all leading to suchness, that they will lead to suchness, and that they have led to suchness.**

In the final analysis, the Buddha's teachings are directly or indirectly related to suchness. The texts that obviously deal with impermanence, suffering, and so forth, also ultimately deal with suchness, for although they expound gross selflessness, such as the non-duality of subject and object, they lead directly to that subtle emptiness that the Buddha taught directly during the second Turning of the Wheel of Dharma.

> **One way of doing this meditation is to set the mind closely on the mental and physical aggregates, as an object that includes all phenomena. Another way is to place the mind on an image of the Buddha. The *King of Meditative Stabilization Sutra* says:**
>
> > **With his body gold in color,**
> > **The lord of the universe is extremely beautiful.**
> > **The Bodhisattva who places his mind on this object**
> > **Is referred to as one in meditative absorption.**

There are various objects of calm abiding meditation. The tantric systems are unique in employing a meditational deity or seed-syllable as the object. Here, as taught in the sutra system, the

Buddha's image is used as the object. Meditative stabilization is a practice common to Buddhists and non-Buddhists. Therefore, it is advisable for a Buddhist to take the image of a Buddha as the object of meditation. In this way he or she will reap a number of incidental benefits, such as accumulating merit and remembering the Buddha. Visualize the image of the Buddha seated on a throne of precious jewels. It should be approximately the full length of your body away from you, abiding in the space in front of you at the level of your forehead. You should imagine that the image is both dense and radiant.

The intelligent practitioner seeks concentration by first gaining a proper understanding of the view. Such a person focuses on emptiness as the object of meditation and aims to actualize calm abiding in this way. This is indeed difficult. Others use the mind itself as the object in their quest for calm abiding. The meditator in fact focuses on clarity and awareness, which is a way for the mind to focus on itself. This is not an easy task either. Initially a practitioner needs to identify clear awareness as an actual experience. The mind then focuses on that feeling with the help of mindfulness. Mind is mysterious and has myriad appearances. It cannot be identified in the way external objects can. It has no shape, form, or color. This mere clear awareness is of the nature of experience and feeling. It is something like colored water—although the water is not of the same nature as the color, so long as they are mixed the true color of the water is not obvious. Similarly, the mind does not have the nature of external objects such as physical form, and so forth. However, the mind is so habituated to following the five sensory consciousnesses that it becomes almost indistinguishable from the physical form, shape, color, and so forth, that it experiences.

In this context, the mode of meditation is to deliberately stop all kinds of thoughts and perceptions. You start by restraining the mind from following the sensory consciousnesses. This should be followed by stopping the mind that reflects on sensory experiences and feelings of joy and misery. Focus the mind on its present and natural state without allowing it to become preoccupied with memories of the past or plans for the future. Through such a process the mind's true color, so to speak, will gradually dawn on the practitioner. When the mind is free from all kinds of thoughts and concepts, suddenly a form of vacuity will appear. If the meditator tries to gain familiarity with that vacuity, the clarity of the consciousness will naturally become more obvious.

Throughout the process of practicing calm abiding meditation, we should be fully aware of the five defects and the eight antidotes. The five defects are laziness, forgetting the object of meditation, mental dullness and excitement, not applying the antidote when afflicted by mental dullness or excitement, and unnecessary application of the antidotes. Let me identify the eight antidotes. They are faith, interest, perseverance, pliancy, mindfulness, conscientiousness, application of the antidotes when afflicted by dullness or excitement, and discarding unnecessary application of the antidotes. Faith here refers to the delight or joy in the practice of concentration that arises from appreciating its benefits. This naturally leads to interest in the practice and helps enhance perseverance. The first four antidotes—faith, interest, perseverance, and pliancy—counteract laziness, and the fifth antidote, mindfulness, counteracts forgetting the object of meditation. Conscientiousness, the sixth antidote, is the opponent of dullness and excitement. When the mind suffers from dullness, effort should be made to awaken and uplift the mind. Excitement should be countered by calming down the agitated mind. Through prolonged practice, the meditator gains mental stability and ascends through the stages of concentration. On the eighth and ninth stages the mind is in profound concentration. At that time, application of the antidotes is only a distraction, and so should be avoided.

> **In this way place the mind on the object of your choice and, having done so, repeatedly and continuously place the mind. Having placed the mind in this way, examine it and check whether it is properly focused on the object. Also check for dullness and see whether the mind is being distracted to external objects.**

With respect to developing calm abiding meditation, the practitioner is at liberty to choose the object of meditation that he or she feels to be appropriate and comfortable. He or she should then concentrate the mind on the object, not allowing it to become distracted to external objects, nor letting it fall into the pits of dullness. He or she should aim to attain single-pointed concentration conjoined with sharp clarity.

Dullness occurs when the mind is dominated by laziness, and lacks alertness and sharpness. Even in everyday life we may describe our minds as "unclear" or "sluggish." When dullness is present, the meditator is not holding firmly onto the object, and so the meditation is not effective.

If the mind is found to be dull due to sleepiness and mental torpor or if you fear that dullness is approaching, then the mind should attend to a supremely delightful object such as an image of the Buddha, or a notion of light. In this process, having dispelled dullness the mind should try to see the object very clearly.

Mental torpor and dullness occur in a mutual cause-and-effect relationship. When a meditator is beset by fogginess, the mind and body feel heavy. The practitioner loses clarity, and the mind becomes functionally ineffective and unproductive. Dullness is a form of mental depression, so to counteract it employ techniques that can help uplift the mind. Some of the more effective ways are to think about joyful objects, such as the wonderful qualities of a Buddha, or to think about the rarity of the precious human life and the opportunities it provides. You should draw inspiration from these thoughts to engage in a fruitful meditation.

In developing calm abiding, the other main obstacle to be overcome is mental excitement. This occurs when the mind is in a state of excitement, chasing the objects of desire and recalling past experiences of joy and happiness. Grosser forms of mental excitement will cause the mind to lose the object of concentration completely: in subtler forms only a portion of the mind attends to the object. The solution to this problem is to meditate on impermanence, suffering, and so forth, which can help the mind to settle down.

You should recognize the presence of dullness when the mind cannot see the object very clearly, when you feel as if you are blind or in a dark place or that you

> **have closed your eyes. If, while you are in meditation, your mind chases after qualities of external objects such as form, or turns its attention to other phenomena, or is distracted by desire for an object you have previously experienced, or if you suspect distraction is approaching, reflect that all composite phenomena are impermanent. Think about suffering and so forth, topics that will temper the mind.**

If you contemplate the faults of constant mental distraction, or any other object that would discourage your mind, you will be able to reduce mental excitement. When the mind loses the object of meditation and becomes distracted by thoughts of your past experiences, particularly in relation to objects of attachment, it is called excitement. When the mind completely loses the object of meditation and becomes distracted by actual external objects, it is gross excitement. If the mind has not lost the object of meditation, but a part of the mind dwells on an object of attachment, it is called subtle excitement. Excitement arises when the mind is too buoyant. When the mind is too buoyant and overly active, it is easily distracted. The antidote to this is to dampen down the mind's high spirits, which can be done by withdrawing the mind. To do that, meditation on objects that reduce obsession and attachment toward external and internal objects is very helpful. And in this context, meditation on impermanence, suffering, and so forth is once again very useful.

The antidote to mental dullness and excitement is introspection. The function of introspection is to observe whether or not the mind is abiding stably on the object of meditation.

The function of mindfulness is to keep the mind on the object; once this is achieved, mental introspection has to watch whether the mind remains on the object or not. The stronger your mindfulness, the stronger your mental introspection will be. For example, if you constantly remember, "It is not good to do this," "This is not helpful," and so forth, you are maintaining introspection. It is important to be mindful of the negative aspects of your daily life and you should be alert to their occurrence. Therefore, one of the unique features and functions of mental introspection is to assess the condition of your mind and body, to judge whether the mind remains stably on the object or not.

At the same time, it is important to remember that if your spirits sink too low, your mind will become dull. At the onset of mental dullness you should make efforts to lift your spirits. Whether you are low spirited or high spirited at any given time depends very much on your health, diet, the time of day, and so forth. So you are the best judge of when to reduce your mental spirits and when to heighten them.

> **In this process, distraction should be eliminated and with the rope of mindfulness and alertness the elephant-like mind should be fastened to the tree of the object of meditation. When you find that the mind is free of dullness and excitement and that it naturally abides on the object, you should relax your effort and remain neutral as long as it continues thus.**

Initially, the mind barely attends to the object of meditation. But with prolonged practice, by developing the antidotes to mental dullness and excitement, the grosser types of these impediments decrease in strength and the subtle types become more obvious. If you persist in the practice and improve the force of your mindfulness and alertness, there will come a time when even the subtle types of these impediments do not obscure your meditation. Generating a strong will to engage in a proper meditation, free of all the obstacles, can have a very positive impact. Eventually you should be able to sit effortlessly for a session of an hour or so.

Realization of single-pointed concentration is not an easy task. You must have the endurance to practice for a long time. By continuous practice you can gradually eliminate the defects of the body and mind. Defects in this context refer to the states of dullness and heaviness of the body and mind that make them unresponsive or unserviceable for meditation. These defects are thoroughly eliminated as the meditator develops the nine stages of calm abiding. The practitioner eventually generates mental pliancy, which is followed by physical pliancy.

> **You should understand that calm abiding is actualized when you enjoy physical and mental pliancy through prolonged familiarity with the meditation, and the mind gains the power to engage the object as it chooses.**

Calm abiding meditation is a practice common to Buddhists and non-Buddhists. So in terms of its mere identity there is nothing profound or special about it. However, when we investigate the nature of some object, whether it is conventional or ultimate, calm abiding meditation is very important. Its main objective is to develop single-pointed concentration. Although we say prayers or engage in tantric practices, we are faced with the question of whether they are effective. The main reason is our lack of concentration. So, we should develop a mind that is able to abide single-pointedly on the object of focus. In the initial stages, even if we are unable to generate a final calmly abiding mind, it is crucial to cultivate a good deal of mental stability while practicing the six perfections, altruistic ideals, and so forth. The final goal of practicing calm abiding meditation is to actualize special insight.

Chapter 9

Actualizing Special Insight

In this text we are talking about engaging in the practice of the six perfections as cultivated by a Bodhisattva. In this context, the purpose of calm abiding meditation is to be able to cultivate a transcendental special insight. Therefore, after having cultivated calm abiding we should endeavor to cultivate special insight.

> **After realizing calm abiding, meditate on special insight, thinking as follows: All the teachings of the Buddha are perfect teachings, and they directly or indirectly reveal and lead to suchness with utmost clarity. If you understand suchness, you will be free of all the nets of wrong views, just as darkness is dispelled when light appears. Mere calm abiding meditation cannot purify pristine awareness, nor can it eliminate the darkness of obscurations. When I meditate properly on suchness with wisdom, pristine awareness will be purified. Only with wisdom can I realize suchness. Only with wisdom can I effectively eradicate obscurations.**

Therefore, engaging in calm abiding meditation I shall search for suchness with wisdom. And I shall not remain content with calm abiding alone.

The altruistic thought that aspires to the highest enlightenment is generated on the basis of compassion. Having strongly established such an altruistic motivation, the practitioner engages in virtuous activities such as calm abiding meditation and special insight.

Now, let us discuss meditation on special insight. In order to meditate on the special insight that realizes ultimate reality, we need to develop the wisdom that understands selflessness. Before we can do that, we must search for and identify the self that does not exist. We cannot be satisfied with merely believing in its absence. We must ascertain from the depths of our heart that there is no basis for such a self to exist. It is possible to reach this ascertainment by way of bare perception or by reasoning, just as we ascertain any other phenomenon, secular or religious. If an object is tangible, we do not have to prove its existence, because we can see and touch it. But with regard to obscure phenomena, we have to use logic and lines of reasoning to establish their existence.

Selflessness is of two types: the selflessness of persons and the selflessness of phenomena. So the self to be negated is also of two types: the self of persons and the self of phenomena. A person is defined in relation to the mental and physical aggregates. But to ordinary perception, the self, or person, appears to be the ruler over the body and mind. The person thus appears to possess a self-sufficient entity or self that does not have to rely on the mental and physical aggregates, their continuity, or their parts and so forth. That notion of a self-sufficient person, which we ordinarily cling to very strongly, is the self of persons we are seeking to identify. It is the self to be negated. Through intellectual processes a practitioner can come to understand that such a self does not exist. At that point he or she develops the wisdom understanding the selflessness of persons.

The selflessness of phenomena refers to the perceived object's lacking true existence and the perceiving mind's lacking true existence. Perceived objects are of the nature of the perceiving mind, but normally they appear to exist externally. When we cling to that external existence, it becomes the basis for developing attachment and aversion. On the other hand, when we see the reality that perceived objects are devoid of external existence and that they are merely of the nature of the perceiving mind, then the force of desire and animosity are naturally reduced. The perceived object's lacking external existence, and the perceiver and the perceived object's lacking separate identity or substance, constitute the grosser level of the selflessness of phenomena.

The perceiving mind, too, is devoid of true existence. When we say things lack true existence, we mean that things exist under the sway of the mind to which they appear, and that objects do not have a unique or substantial existence from their own side. To our mistaken mind things appear to exist from their own side, and we cling to that appearance. But in actuality things are empty of such an existence. This is the subtle emptiness according to this school. Thus, by negating the apparent true existence of things, we develop a sense of their illusory nature. Understanding the reality that things are like illusions counters the generation of negative emotions like attachment and aversion.

Here the author very clearly explains that all the teachings of the Buddha are ultimately intended as instructions to guide practitioners toward realizing the state of enlightenment. In pursuit of this goal, an understanding of suchness is crucial. The Buddha himself achieved enlightenment by actualizing the meaning of ultimate truth. There are countless philosophical views, but if we follow correct views, we can make progress on the spiritual path and gain insight into ultimate truth. On the other hand, following incorrect views leads to the wrong paths and unpleasant consequences. Practitioners who gain proper insight into the view of suchness can thoroughly eliminate all their wrong views from the very root.

> **What is suchness like? It is the nature of all phenomena that ultimately they are empty of the self of persons and the self of phenomena. This is realized through the perfection of wisdom and not otherwise. The *Unraveling of the Thought Sutra* reads, "'O Tathagata, by which perfection do Bodhisattvas apprehend the identitylessness of phenomena?' 'Avalokiteshvara, it is apprehended by the perfection of wisdom.'" Therefore, meditate on wisdom while engaging in calm abiding.**

Suchness refers to the selflessness of both persons and phenomena, but mainly to the selflessness of phenomena. When expounding it in detail, scholars differ in their interpretations. According to this text, the selflessness of phenomena is described as subtler than the selflessness of persons. A person is posited in reliance upon the mental and physical aggregates. When we talk about the selflessness of a person, the person refers to a self-sufficient person existing in its own right, without relying on the aggregates. Such a person does not exist even on a conventional level, and therefore to be devoid of such an identity is what is known as the selflessness of persons.

The great Kamalashila, a renowned student of the esteemed Shantarakshita, belonged to the Yogachara Svatantrika Madhyamika school of thought. This school asserted two levels of the selflessness of phenomena—subtle and gross. The non-duality of subject and object, or perceiver and perceived, is the gross level of suchness, while seeing all phenomena as empty of true existence is the subtle level of suchness. Of all the sutras the Buddha taught, the Perfection of Wisdom sutras deal with this subject in greatest depth.

It is extremely important that the notion of "I," the selflessness of persons, and the selflessness of phenomena be scrutinized thoroughly. Each of us has an innate and spontaneous feeling of "I." This is what experiences happiness and sorrow, and also what gives rise to happiness and sorrow. Different schools of thought have posited various views since ancient times on the way in which the "I" exists. One of the ancient Indian philosophical schools viewed the self or "I" as the user, and the mental and physical aggregates as the objects to be used. Thus, the self and the aggregates are viewed as different entities.

According to other philosophers, the self is a permanent, single, and independent entity. The self is what has come from previous lives and what travels to the next when the mental and physical aggregates disintegrate at the time of death. I have the impression that other religions like Christianity also believe in a self that is permanent, single, and independent. By implication, such a self does not depend or rely on its aggregates. None of the four schools of thought within Buddhism believe in such a self. They deny the self's having any substantial existence apart from the mental and physical aggregates.

Nevertheless, according to Buddhist philosophy, the self does exist. If we were to contend that the self does not exist at all, we would plainly contradict common perception. We should examine and analyze the way in which the self does exist. Through logical analysis we can determine that the self exists in dependence on the mental and physical aggregates. Different schools provide different levels of interpretation of the aggregates, but it is generally agreed that the perception of the self is formed by relying on the perception of the aggregates. In other words, the existence of the self can only be posited in reliance upon the aggregates.

Why make the effort to search for the self, or "I," and investigate the nature of its existence? By and large we think of people as belonging to two camps: those belonging to our own side and those belonging to the other side. We are attached to those on our side and we generate animosity toward those on the other side. Motivated by attachment and animosity, we commit various negative actions of body, speech, and mind. At the root of all these unwholesome and unhealthy thoughts and actions lies the feeling of "I," or self. The intensity and scope of our negative actions depend on how strongly we hold to the misconception of self. It is important to realize that this clinging onto the "I" is innate, and yet when we search and try to pinpoint the "I," we cannot find a self-sufficient "I" that has control over the mental and physical aggregates.

Because of this innate misconception of the "I," we have an endless succession of desires. Some of these desires are very peculiar. An ordinary person recognizes someone else's physical beauty or intelligence, and desires to exchange them for his or her own inferior qualities. The true mode of existence of the self is that it is imputed in relation to its causes and other factors. We are not trying to negate the sense of a self, or "I," as such, but we should definitely be able to reduce the strength and intensity of our sense of a self-sufficient "self."

> **Yogis should analyze in the following manner: a person is not observed as separate from the mental and physical aggregates, the elements and sense powers. Nor is a person of the nature of the aggregates and so forth, because the aggregates and so forth have the entity of being many and impermanent. Others have imputed the person as permanent and single. The person as a phenomenon cannot exist except as one or many, because there is no other way of existing. Therefore, we must conclude that the assertion of the worldly "I" and "mine" is wholly mistaken.**

There is no self or person existing in isolation from the mental and physical aggregates. This is to say that a person exists in reliance upon the aggregates. This can be well understood by observing our everyday conventions. When the body and other aggregates are young, we say the person is young; when they age, we say the person is old. These conventional expressions concur with the actuality that the person exists in dependence on the aggregates.

> **Meditation on the selflessness of phenomena should also be done in the following manner: phenomena, in short, are included under the five aggregates, the twelve sources of perception, and the eighteen elements. The physical aspects of the aggregates, sources of perception, and elements are, in the ultimate sense, nothing other than aspects of the mind. This is because when they are broken into subtle particles and the nature of the parts of these subtle particles is individually examined, no definite identity can be found.**

"Phenomena" here refers to everything that is enjoyed or used by a person, such as the five mental and physical aggregates, twelve sensory sources, and eighteen elements. All these external objects, such as physical form and so forth, appear to have an identity separate from the perceiving mind. But in reality this is not the case. If they possessed an identity separate from the perceiving mind, then the two, the phenomenon and the perceiving mind, should by definition be wholly unrelated entities. This would also contradict the notion that things are posited by the perceiving mind. The object perceived does not have an identity separate from the mind that perceives it. If things like physical form were to have external existence, we should be able to find it even after we had removed the form's component parts piece-by-piece. Since this is not the case, we can conclude that things are devoid of external existence. This also implies that the perceived object and the perceiving mind do not exist as separate entities. Therefore, proponents of this school of thought say that there is no external existence apart from being of the same nature as the mind.

Ordinary people have misconceived physical form over beginningless time, therefore forms and so forth appear to be separate and external to the mind, just like the physical forms that appear in dreams. In the ultimate sense, physical form and so forth are nothing other than aspects of the mind.

Thus, suchness, or emptiness, refers to a lack of substantial separation between the subjective mind and the object perceived by that mind. This is because when physical things are broken into small particles and the identity of those particles is sought, no definite identity, or self, can be pinpointed. This view of the Chittamatra, or Mind Only School, is very similar to the contention of the Yogachara Svatantrika Madhyamika, with some subtle differences, but this view is not acceptable to the later Madhyamika schools. So, the next lines explain the exclusive philosophical viewpoint of the Madhyamika.

> **In the ultimate sense, the mind too cannot be real. How can the mind that apprehends only the false nature of physical form and so forth, and appears in various aspects, be real? Just as physical forms and so forth are false, since the mind does not exist separately from physical forms and so forth, which are false, it too is false. Just as physical forms and so forth possess various aspects, and their identities are neither one nor many, similarly, since the mind is not different from**

them, its identity too is neither one nor many. Therefore, the mind by nature is like an illusion.

Even among Buddhist schools of thought, the interpretation of the meaning of emptiness differs. The interpretation of the Chittamatra School is not acceptable to those who propound the Madhyamika philosophy; likewise, the proponents of the Chittamatra School too have their own logic to refute the Madhyamika viewpoint. We need to develop a broad perspective enabling us to see the wholeness of the Buddhist philosophy rather than its fragments. The views presented by the lower schools should directly or indirectly aid the practitioner in realizing the views of the higher schools. The above passage deals with the selflessness of phenomena as it is presented exclusively by the Madhyamika School. According to this school, every phenomenon is a mere label imputed by the mind. It is not only external existence, but the mind that perceives the various categories of false phenomena that is devoid of true existence. In this way the Madhyamikas assert that all phenomena, external or internal, lack true existence, or do not exist ultimately. When things appear to the mind, they appear to exist truly, but in reality they lack such an identity. There is a discrepancy between the way things appear and the way they exist. Such a discrepancy is unacceptable as the ultimate nature of a phenomenon. Therefore, all phenomena are devoid of true existence.

Analyze that, just like the mind, the nature of all phenomena, too, is like an illusion. In this way, when the identity of the mind is specifically examined by

wisdom, in the ultimate sense it is perceived neither within nor without. It is also not perceived in the absence of both. Neither the mind of the past, nor that of the future, nor that of the present, is perceived. When the mind is born, it comes from nowhere, and when it ceases it goes nowhere because it is inapprehensible, undemonstrable, and non-physical. If you ask, "What is the entity of that which is inapprehensible, undemonstrable, and non-physical?" the *Heap of Jewels* states: "O Kashyapa, when the mind is thoroughly sought, it cannot be found. What is not found cannot be perceived. And what is not perceived is neither past nor future nor present." Through such analysis, the beginning of the mind is ultimately not seen, the end of the mind is ultimately not seen, and the middle of the mind is ultimately not seen.

All phenomena should be understood as lacking an end and a middle, just as the mind does not have an end or a middle. With the knowledge that the mind is without an end or a middle, no identity of the mind is perceived. What is thoroughly realized by the mind, too, is realized as being empty. By realizing that, the very identity, which is established as the aspect of the mind, like the identity of physical form, and so forth, is also ultimately not perceived. In this way, when the person does not ultimately see the identity of all phenomena through wisdom, he will not analyze whether physical form is permanent or impermanent, empty or not empty, contaminated or not contaminated, produced or non-produced, and existent or non-existent. Just as physical form is not examined, similarly feeling,

recognition, compositional factors, and consciousness are not examined. When the object does not exist, its characteristics also cannot exist. So how can they be examined?

The above passage deals with ultimate reality; its meaning is that in the ultimate sense the object of imputation is not findable. In this context we find in the *Heart Sutra* phrases like: "There is no physical form, no sound, no smell, no taste, and no object of touch." The mind, too, is not findable in the ultimate sense. Since in the ultimate sense such things are non-existent, there is no point examining whether they are permanent or impermanent. Ultimately all phenomena, including the aggregates and so forth, are devoid of true existence. Within the notion of ultimate reality, things are devoid of true existence. In the same way, suchness, which is an attribute of phenomena, is also devoid of true existence. This is important. Even when we understand that phenomena like physical form and so forth are devoid of true existence, there is a danger of thinking that ultimate reality may have true existence.

In this way, when the person does not firmly apprehend the entity of a thing as ultimately existing, having investigated it with wisdom, the practitioner engages in non-conceptual single-pointed concentration. And thus the identitylessness of all phenomena is realized.

The above passage conveys what it means to realize selflessness. The wisdom realizing selflessness must ascertain selflessness; it is not simply a matter of no longer having any misconceptions about the self. For example, the mind conceives of things like physical form in various ways. There is a mind that conceives of physical form as having true existence, another that conceives of it as having the attributes of true existence, yet another that conceives of it with attributes lacking true existence, and again one that conceives of it without assigning it any attributes of true existence or non-true existence. So, the analyzing wisdom must discern the self to be refuted. After refuting that self, its opposite, selflessness, will be actualized.

> **Those who do not meditate with wisdom by analyzing the entity of things specifically, but merely meditate on the elimination of mental activity, cannot avert conceptual thoughts and also cannot realize identitylessness because they lack the light of wisdom. If the fire of consciousness knowing phenomena as they are is produced from individual analysis of suchness, then like the fire produced by rubbing wood it will burn the wood of conceptual thought. The Buddha has spoken in this way.**

In order to understand the true nature of things, it is vital that a practitioner use intelligence and wisdom in the process of examination. As the author clearly states, the mere elimination of mental activity does not constitute meditation on suchness. When mentally inactive, an individual may not be misconceiving the self, but he or she also lacks any sense of discerning selflessness; this sheds no light, and so the individual is not free from the fabrications of misconceptions. Therefore, we need to generate sparks of wisdom that enable us to fathom selflessness.

> The *Cloud of Jewels* also states, "One skilled in discerning the faults engages in the yoga of meditation on emptiness in order to get rid of all conceptual elaborations. Such a person, due to his repeated meditation on emptiness, when he thoroughly searches for the object and the identity of the object, which delights the mind and distracts it, realizes them to be empty. When that very mind is also examined, it is realized to be empty. When the identity of what is realized by this mind is thoroughly sought, this too is realized as empty. Realizing in this way one enters into the yoga of signlessness." This shows that only those who have engaged in complete analysis can enter into the yoga of signlessness.
>
> It has been explained very clearly that through mere elimination of mental activity, without examining the identity of things with wisdom, it is not possible to engage in non-conceptual meditation. Thus, concentration is done after the actual identity of things like physical form and so forth has been perfectly analyzed with wisdom, and not by concentrating on physical form and so forth. Concentration is also not done by abiding between this world and the world beyond, because physical forms and so forth are not perceived. It is thus called the non-abiding concentration.
>
> [Such a practitioner] is then called a meditator of supreme wisdom, because by specifically examining the identity of all things with wisdom he has perceived nothing. This is as stated in the *Space Treasure Sutra* and the *Jewel in the Crown Sutra*, and so forth.

When it is investigated, the perceiving mind is understood to be empty and the objects of the mind are also empty of true existence. A practitioner with such knowledge engages in what is known as the signless yoga. In the ultimate sense, all imputed phenomena, including objects of perception such as physical form, and the perceiving mind are all empty of self-identity. It is important to note that in order to enter into non-conceptual absorption it is crucial to engage in thorough analysis first. When the objects of imputation are sought by discerning wisdom, nothing is findable. The true meaning of understanding selflessness needs to be appreciated in perspective. Mere lack of mental activity does not constitute understanding selflessness. Mere absence of a misconception of self does not imply a knowledge of selflessness. Selflessness is understood by the wisdom that finds that both the perceiving mind and the perceived objects lack any self-identity in the ultimate sense. This knowledge dawns on the practitioner after thorough and discerning scrutiny and analysis.

> **In this way, by entering into the suchness of the selflessness of persons and phenomena, you are free from concepts and analysis because there is nothing to be thoroughly examined and observed. You are free from expression, and with single-pointed mental engagement you automatically enter into meditation without exertion. Thus, you very clearly meditate on suchness and abide in it. While abiding in that meditation, the continuity of the mind should not be distracted. When the mind is distracted to external objects due to attachment, and so forth, such distraction should be noted. Quickly pacify the distraction by meditating on the repulsive aspect of such objects and swiftly replace the mind on suchness.**

> **If the mind appears to be disinclined to do that, reflecting on the advantages of single-pointed concentration, meditate with delight. The disinclination should be pacified by also seeing the defects of distraction.**
>
> **If the function of the mind becomes unclear and starts sinking, or when there is a risk of it sinking due to being overpowered by mental torpor or sleep, then as before, quickly attempt to overcome such dullness by focusing the mind on supremely delightful things. Then the object suchness should be held in very tight focus. At times when the mind is observed to be excited or tempted to become distracted by the memory of past events of laughter and play, then as in the earlier cases, pacify the distraction by reflecting on such things as impermanence, and so forth, which will help subdue the mind. Then, again endeavor to engage the mind on suchness without applying counter forces.**

These lines explain the method of meditation on special insight with respect to ultimate reality. The mind that single-pointedly concentrates on suchness sees nothing but vacuity after rejecting the object of to be refuted. Nothing appears to that mind except vacuity. The mind that is absorbed in selflessness discards the basis of all misconceptions. It is therefore referred to as one that is free of concepts and analysis, a single-pointed mind beyond expression. When the mind single-pointedly meditates on suchness, it is described as "absorbed in suchness" and "entering suchness." When clarity is gained through prolonged practice, the meditation should be continued without distraction. Seeing selflessness but once is not enough, you should make effort to maintain the momentum of understanding. The meditation on special insight is developed by force of analytical wisdom, and by the power of such analysis mental and physical ecstasy will be generated.

As discussed before in the context of calm abiding meditation, the practitioner should be aware of the interfering forces such as mental excitement and dullness. In the process of analytical meditation, when you lose the clarity of the object, the mind is distracted to other objects. When the sharpness or intensity wanes, dullness has arisen. When these impediments obstruct your meditation, you should apply the necessary antidotes. In this respect Kamalashila clearly states that when the mind is distracted by external objects as a result of desire, you should meditate on repulsive aspects of the object and on impermanence. When the practitioner's mind, under the sway of mental torpor and sleep, lacks clarity, he or she should meditate on supremely delightful objects such as an image of the Buddha. By applying such antidotes, interfering forces will be pacified and your meditation enhanced.

> **If and when the mind spontaneously engages in meditation on suchness, free of sinking and mental agitation, it should be left naturally and your efforts should be relaxed. If effort is applied when the mind is in meditative equipoise, it will distract the mind. But if effort is not applied when the mind becomes dull, it will become like a blind man due to extreme dullness and you will not achieve special insight. So, when the mind becomes dull, apply effort, and when in absorption, effort should be relaxed. When, by meditating**

> **on special insight, excessive wisdom is generated and calm abiding is weak, the mind will waver like a butter lamp in the wind and you will not perceive suchness very clearly. Therefore, at that time meditate on calm abiding. When calm abiding meditation becomes excessive, meditate on wisdom.**

Here the author has explained in clear and lucid terms that when the practitioner can single-pointedly place the mind on suchness, free of mental dullness and excitement, he or she should continue the meditation. After analysis by the wisdom understanding suchness, if you can maintain the placement of the mind on suchness, the meditation should be allowed to follow its natural course. When meditation is free of mental agitation and dullness, application of the antidotes will only be counterproductive.

Until you achieve special insight into suchness, it is vital to maintain a balance between the analytical and concentrative meditations. Through analytical meditation, you will gain an understanding of selflessness. The strength of this knowledge should be complemented by single-pointed concentration. Over-analysis harms concentration, and excessive concentration detracts from analytical wisdom. So practice a harmonious blend of the two types of meditation. Gradually you will attain the union of special insight and calm abiding meditation.

Chapter 10

Unifying Method and Wisdom

> **When both are equally engaged, keep still, effortlessly, so long as there is no physical or mental discomfort. If physical or mental discomfort arises, see the whole world like an illusion, a mirage, a dream, a reflection of the moon in water, and an apparition. And think: "These sentient beings are very troubled in the cycle of existence due to their not understanding such profound knowledge." Then, generate great compassion and the awakening mind of bodhichitta, thinking: "I shall earnestly endeavor to help them understand suchness." Take rest. Again, in the same way, engage in a single-pointed concentration on the non-appearance of all phenomena. If the mind is discouraged, then similarly take rest. This is the path of engaging in a union of calm abiding meditation and special insight. It focuses on the image conceptually and non-conceptually.**

Here the text explains how to achieve special insight after having achieved calm abiding. From that point on you can engage in the practice of the union of special insight and calm abiding meditation. In other words, you engage in the practice of both single-pointed meditation and analytical meditation. While practicing these meditations, it is wise not to be overenthusiastic. You should take care of your physical and mental health. The meditation session should not be too long. Before sitting down to meditate you should gather whatever you need to protect your body from extremes of heat and cold. When you become tired from long meditation sessions, you should take a rest from single-pointed meditation and think of all phenomena as like illusions or mirages and so forth. You can also think about compassion for all beings confused in the cycle of existence. With such wholesome thoughts, motivate yourself to help sentient beings to realize the nature of reality.

Again take rest and then resume the practice of concentration on the non-appearance of all phenomena, which refers to meditation on selflessness. This is because when you meditate single-pointedly on selflessness, conventional phenomena cease to appear to your mind. If your mind becomes weary as a result of such meditation, you should again take rest. Then once more continue your meditation on the union of special insight and calm abiding, which is also known as focusing on the reflection both conceptually and non-conceptually.

> **Thus, through this progress, a yogi should meditate on suchness for an hour, or half a session in the night, or one full session, or for as long as is comfortable. This is the meditative stabilization thoroughly discerning the ultimate, as taught in the *Descent into Lanka Sutra.***

Then, if you wish to arise from the concentration, while your legs are still crossed think as follows: "Although ultimately all these phenomena lack identity, conventionally they definitely exist. If this were not the case, how would the relationship between cause and effect, and so forth, prevail? The Buddha has also said,

> Things are produced conventionally,
> But ultimately they lack intrinsic identity.

Sentient beings with a childish attitude exaggerate phenomena, thinking of them as having an intrinsic identity when they lack it. Thus attributing intrinsic existence to those things that lack it confuses their minds, and they wander in the cycle of existence for a long time. For these reasons, I shall endeavor without fail to achieve the omniscient state by accomplishing the unsurpassable accumulations of merit and insight in order to help them realize suchness."

Then slowly arise from the cross-legged position and make prostrations to the Buddhas and Bodhisattvas of the ten directions. Make them offerings and sing their praises. And make vast prayers by reciting the *Prayer of Noble Conduct,* and so forth. Thereafter, engage in conscious efforts to actualize the accumulations of merit and insight by practicing generosity and so forth, which are endowed with the essence of emptiness and great compassion.

After you have arisen from meditative absorption, make proper dedication prayers. The practitioner should place equal emphasis on generosity and other practices during the post-meditation period. During that time, dependent origination and emptiness must be understood as interchangeable. Emptiness in this context means that things lack their own intrinsic self-identity; it does not mean non-existence. Therefore it does not cause a fall into the extreme of nihilism. One who properly fathoms the Middle Way view of Madhyamika philosophy naturally eliminates both the extremes. The implication is that when you understand the philosophy of emptiness, there is no contradiction in presenting the law of cause and effect on the conventional level. On the contrary, you gain greater certainty of the workings of the law of cause and effect when your knowledge of emptiness becomes more profound. Emptiness does not mean nothingness; it means that things are empty of intrinsic existence. So, during the post-meditation period, the practitioner should accumulate merit, which will complement the practice of insight during the meditation.

> **If you act thus, your meditative stabilization will actualize that emptiness that possesses the best of all qualities. The *Jewel in the Crown Sutra* states, "Donning the armor of loving-kindness, while abiding in the state of great compassion, practice meditative stabilization that actualizes the emptiness possessing the best of all qualities. What is the emptiness possessing the best of all qualities? It is that which is not divorced from generosity, ethics, patience, effort, meditative stabilization, wisdom, or skillful means." Bodhisattvas must rely on virtuous practices like generosity as means to thoroughly ripen all sentient beings and in order to perfect the place, body, and manifold retinue.**

Supreme emptiness refers to the wisdom that directly realizes emptiness and is supported by the practice of the method aspects.

Note that practice of generosity and the other perfections is essential. This is because the fully enlightened state of Buddhahood is produced by the realization of favorable causes and conditions. There is no causeless production and nothing is produced by contrary causes. A Bodhisattva has many wonderful advantages to help enhance the welfare of sentient beings; every virtue performed by such a noble being is very powerful and effective. Therefore, Bodhisattvas earnestly engage in the practice of the method aspects of the path, including the six perfections, in order to swiftly actualize the state of Buddhahood.

If it were not so, what would be the causes of these fields, the field of Buddhas and so forth, that the Buddha spoke about? The omniscient wisdom possessing the best of all qualities can be accomplished through generosity and other skillful means. Therefore, the Buddha has said that omniscient wisdom is perfected by skillful means. Therefore, Bodhisattvas should also cultivate generosity and other skillful means and not only emptiness.

The *Extensive Collection of All Qualities Sutra* also says,

> **"O Maitreya, Bodhisattvas thoroughly accomplish the six perfections in order to attain the final fruit of Buddhahood. But to this the foolish respond: 'Bodhisattvas should train only in the perfection of wisdom—what is the need for the rest of the perfections?' They repudiate the other perfections. Maitreya, what do you think of this? When the king of Kashi offered his flesh to the hawk for the sake of a pigeon was it a corruption of wisdom?" Maitreya replied, "This is not so." The Buddha said, "Maitreya,**

> **Bodhisattvas accumulated roots of merit through their deeds in conjunction with the six perfections. Are these roots of merit harmful?" Maitreya replied, "O Buddha, this is not so." The Buddha further spoke, "Maitreya, you have also correctly practiced the perfection of generosity for sixty aeons, the perfection of ethics for sixty aeons, the perfection of patience for sixty aeons, the perfection of enthusiastic perseverance for sixty aeons, the perfection of meditative stabilization for sixty aeons, and the perfection of wisdom for sixty aeons. To this the foolish respond: 'There is only one way to attain Buddhahood, and that is the way of emptiness.' Their practice is completely mistaken."**

This clearly expresses the importance of developing a combination of both method and wisdom. After developing a comprehensive understanding of emptiness, you should meditate in order to gain deep insight into it. Equal emphasis should be placed on putting the method aspect, which includes the six perfections, into practice. A Bodhisattva's final objective is to attain the highest enlightenment, transcending both the travails of the cycle of existence and the complacent peace of nirvana. To this end, their practice must involve a union of method and wisdom.

> **A Bodhisattva possessing wisdom but not skillful means would be like the Hearers, who are unable to engage in the deeds of Buddhas. But they can do so when supported by skillful means. As the *Heap of Jewels* says, "Kashyapa, it is like this. For instance, kings who are supported by ministers can accomplish all their purposes. Similarly, [when] the wisdom of a Bodhisattva is thoroughly supported by skillful means, such**

a Bodhisattva also performs all the activities of a Buddha." The philosophical view of the path of Bodhisattvas is different from the philosophical paths of the non-Buddhists and Hearers. For example, since the philosophical view of the path of non-Buddhists perversely observes a [truly existent] self, and so forth, such a path is completely and always divorced from wisdom. Therefore, they cannot attain liberation.

The Hearers are separated from great compassion and devoid of skillful means. Therefore, they single-mindedly endeavor to achieve nirvana. In their path, Bodhisattvas enshrine wisdom and skillful means, so they endeavor to achieve the non-abiding nirvana. The Bodhisattva path consists of wisdom and skillful means and, therefore, [they] attain the non-abiding nirvana. Because of the power of wisdom, [they] do not fall into the cycle of existence; due to the power of skillful means, [they] do not fall to nirvana.

The *Hill of Gaya Head Sutra* says, "The Bodhisattva path, in short, is twofold. The two are skillful means and wisdom." The *First Among the Supreme and Glorious* also says, "The perfection of wisdom is the mother and expertise in skillful means is the father."

The *Teaching of Vimalakirti* also says, "What is bondage for Bodhisattvas and what is liberation? Upholding a life in the cycle of existence devoid of skillful means is bondage for Bodhisattvas. [But] to lead a life in the cycle of existence with skillful means is liberation. Upholding a life in the cycle of existence devoid of wisdom is bondage for Bodhisattvas. [But] to lead a life in the cycle of existence with wisdom is liberation. Wisdom not conjoined with skillful means is bondage, [but] wisdom conjoined with skillful means is liberation. The skillful means not conjoined with wisdom is bondage, [but] skillful means conjoined with wisdom is liberation."

If a Bodhisattva cultivates mere wisdom, [he] falls to the nirvana desired by Hearers. Thus, it is like bondage. And [he] cannot achieve non-abiding nirvana. So wisdom separated from skillful means is bondage for Bodhisattvas. Therefore, just as a person chilled by the wind seeks the comfort of fire, so a Bodhisattva cultivates the wisdom of emptiness along with skillful means to eliminate the wind of wrong view. [But he] does not [endeavor] to actualize it as the Hearers do. The *Ten Qualities Sutra* says, "O son of good family, it is like this. For instance, a person who is thoroughly devoted to fire, who respects it and regards it as guru, will not think: 'Because I respect, honor, and venerate fire, I should hold it in both hands.' This is because he realizes that to do so would give him physical pain and cause mental discomfort. Similarly, a Bodhisattva also is aware of nirvana, but also does not try to actualize it. This is because he realizes that by doing so he would be turning away from enlightenment."

If he relies merely on skillful means, the Bodhisattva will not transcend the ordinary level and thus there will only be bondage. Therefore, [he] cultivates skillful means along with wisdom. By the power of wisdom, Bodhisattvas can transform even the disturbing emotions into nectar, like poison under a tantric spell. There is no need to express [the goodness] of generosity, and so forth, which leads to naturally elevated states of existence.

Bodhisattvas are skillful and endowed with wisdom. Because of such special qualities there are activities that, when committed by Hearers and Solitary Realizers, could be considered unwholesome, but when performed by Bodhisattvas could greatly help them to enhance the welfare of other beings. In order to benefit other sentient beings, they do not have to strictly adhere to the rules governing the actions of body and speech.

> The *Heap of Jewels* states, "Kashyapa, it is like this. Due to the power of Tantra and medicine, a poison may not cause death. Similarly, since the disturbing emotions of Bodhisattvas are under the power of wisdom, they cannot cause them downfalls. Therefore, due to the power of skillful means Bodhisattvas do not abandon the cycle of existence; they do not fall to nirvana. Due to the power of wisdom, [they] eliminate all objects [misconceived as truly existent] and therefore [they] do not fall into the cycle of existence. Thus, they attain the non-abiding nirvana of Buddhahood alone." The *Space Treasure Sutra* also says, "Because of the knowledge of wisdom, Bodhisattvas eliminate all disturbing emotions, and due to their knowledge of skillful means they do not abandon sentient beings." The *Unraveling of the Thought Sutra* also says, "I have not taught that someone who is not concerned for the welfare of sentient beings and who is not inclined to realize the nature of all composite phenomena will achieve unsurpassable and perfectly accomplished Buddhahood." Therefore, those interested in Buddhahood must cultivate both wisdom and skillful means.

Bodhisattvas are endowed with great wisdom. So their disturbing emotions become ineffective and do not become causes to propel them into undesirable realms. Since these noble beings strive to develop skillful means and wisdom equally, they are neither overwhelmed by the cycle of existence nor do they fall into the complacent state of nirvana. They are constantly aware of the well being of sentient beings and at the same time aim to achieve the highest enlightenment.

> **While you are meditating on transcendental wisdom or while you are in a deep meditative absorption, you cannot engage in skillful means such as practicing generosity. But skillful means can be cultivated along with wisdom during the preparatory and post-meditative periods. That is the way to engage in wisdom and skillful means simultaneously.**

The wisdom that is direct insight into emptiness is completely free of duality, and the mind is fully absorbed in emptiness like water being poured into water. Obviously, it is not possible to pursue the practice of skillful means during such a period. Nevertheless, the importance of practicing the wisdom aspect and the method aspect in unison should be understood from the right perspective. During the sessions before and after meditation, an individual can practice compassion, altruism, generosity, and so forth, thus enhancing the power of wisdom.

> **Moreover, this is the path of Bodhisattvas in which they engage in an integrated practice of wisdom and skillful means. This is cultivating the transcendental**

path that is thoroughly imbued with great compassion focusing on all sentient beings. And while practicing skillful means, after arising from meditative absorption, you practice generosity and other skillful means without misconception, like a magician. The *Teaching of Akshayamati Sutra* says, "What are a Bodhisattva's skillful means and what wisdom is actualized? The Bodhisattva's skillful means are thinking and placing the mind closely on sentient beings with great compassion while in meditative absorption. And engaging in meditative equipoise with peace and extreme peace is wisdom." There are many more such references. The *Chapter on Controlling Evil Forces* also says: "Furthermore, the perfect activities of Bodhisattvas refer to conscious efforts by the mind of wisdom and the collection of all meritorious Dharma by the mind of skillful means. The mind of wisdom also leads to selflessness, the non-existence of [inherently existent] sentient beings, and of life, sustenance, and the person. And the mind of skillful means leads to thoroughly ripening all sentient beings." The *Extensive Collection of All Qualities Sutra* also states:

> Just as a magician endeavors
> To let his creation go,
> Since he already knows the [nature of his] creation,
> He has no attachment to it.
> Similarly, the three worlds are like an illusion,
> Which the wise Buddha knew about
> Long before he knew the sentient beings in these worlds
> And had undertaken efforts to help them.

It is because of the Bodhisattva's practice of wisdom and skillful means that it is said: In their activities they remain in the cycle of existence, but in their thoughts they abide in nirvana.

For instance, a magician has created a projection of someone in prison. He then attempts to free the person from imprisonment. Since he knows that what he has projected is only an illusion, he has no feeling of attachment or otherwise. In a similar fashion, Buddhas see all sentient beings in the three worlds as like illusions. They do not cling to things as having intrinsic existence and they possess the wisdom realizing that things are empty like an illusion. At the same time, they engage in fulfilling the well being of all sentient beings.

In this way, become familiar with generosity and other skillful means that are dedicated to unsurpassable and perfectly accomplished enlightenment, having the essence of emptiness and great compassion. In order to generate the ultimate awakening mind of bodhichitta, as was done earlier, practice calm abiding meditation and special insight as much as you can in regular sessions. As it was taught in the *Pure Field of Engagement Sutra,* always familiarize yourself with skillful means by closely placing mindfulness on the good qualities of Bodhisattvas who work for the welfare of sentient beings at all times.

Those who become familiar with compassion, skillful means, and the awakening mind of bodhichitta in this way will undoubtedly excel in this life. Buddhas and Bodhisattvas will always be seen in dreams, and

other pleasant dreams will also occur, and appreciative gods will protect you. There will be immense accumulation of merit and insight at every moment. Disturbing emotions and other bad states of existence will be purified. You will enjoy much happiness and mental peace at all times and a great many beings will cherish you. Physically, too, you will be free of disease. You will attain supreme mental facility, and thus you will achieve special qualities like clairvoyance.

When you engage in the practice of the teachings, try to gain some intellectual understanding of the view of emptiness. As we discussed earlier, things are devoid of true existence—they do not have a unique existence from their own side. When we recite prayers or make prostrations, we must develop some feeling for the illusory nature of things. Dedications too should be made within the framework of the philosophy of selflessness. Understanding and remembering the meaning of emptiness is equally relevant within tantric practices. Practice of all kinds of virtuous activities in relation to the knowledge of emptiness greatly helps us ascend the spiritual path. At the same time, disturbing emotions and all other defects are reduced and gradually eliminated, while compassion, altruism, skillful means, and other virtues gain strength.

Then you will travel by miraculous power to innumerable worlds, make offerings to the Buddhas and listen to teachings from them. At the time of death, too, you will undoubtedly see Buddhas and Bodhisattvas. In future lives you will be reborn in special families and places, where you will not be separated from Buddhas and Bodhisattvas. Thus, you will effortlessly

accomplish all accumulations of merit and insight. You will have great wealth, a large following, and many attendants. Possessing a sharp intelligence, you will be able to ripen the mindstreams of many beings. In all lives such a person will be able to recall past lives. Try to understand such immeasurable advantages that are also described in other sutras.

In this way, if you meditate on compassion, skillful means, and the awakening mind of bodhichitta for a long time with great admiration, the mindstream will gradually become thoroughly purified and ripened. Then, like producing fire by rubbing together pieces of wood, you will accomplish your meditation on the perfect reality. You will thus achieve an extremely clear knowledge of the sphere of phenomena free from conceptual elaborations, the transcendental wisdom free of the impeding nets of conceptual thought. This wisdom of ultimate bodhichitta is stainless like an unwavering butter lamp undisturbed by the wind. Thus, such a mind in the entity of ultimate bodhichitta is included within the path of seeing, which apprehends the selfless nature of all phenomena. Through this achievement you enter into the path focusing on the reality of things and you are then born in the family of Tathagatas; you enter the stainless state of a Bodhisattva, turn away from all wandering births, abide in the suchness of Bodhisattvas, and attain the first Bodhisattva level. You can find more details of these advantages in other texts such as the *Ten Spiritual Levels.* This is how meditative stabilization focusing on suchness is taught in the *Descent into Lanka Sutra.* This is how Bodhisattvas enter into the non-conceptual meditation free from elaborations.

When we see someone in misery, we feel compassion. We must realize that it is very important to cherish such an attitude and strengthen it with the help of other skillful means. We also have our human intelligence, which gives us the ability to discern what is right and what is wrong. This too should be improved and directed toward discerning the ultimate reality. In achieving these purposes, it is essential to perform meritorious deeds and acts of purification. Fundamentally it is vital to cultivate the faculty of discerning wisdom. With such wisdom examine the ultimate reality over and over again and develop an intellectual appreciation of the meaning of suchness. This in turn will help generate a profound feeling for its reality. This analytical approach should be augmented by meditative concentration. The practice of compassion and the knowledge of emptiness will lead the individual to realize that the impurities of the mind can be removed and the state of omniscience can be achieved.

After prolonged practice of the teachings, with compassion as the foundation complemented by wisdom, an individual will strongly wish to attain the state of Buddhahood. When such a wish for the welfare of all sentient beings is in earnest and comes from the bottom of his or her heart, he or she will become a Bodhisattva and will attain the Mahayana path of accumulation. Of the three levels of this path [small, middling, and great], the small level is attained. This is called the earth-like awakening mind. The awakening mind is of twenty-one types. The practitioner improves the awakening mind as a result of compassion and also strengthens his or her knowledge of emptiness. Calm abiding meditation is practiced in relation to emptiness and when the wisdom deriving from that meditation is generated, the individual attains the path of preparation.

The meditation should be continued, with the awareness that full coordination between the method and wisdom aspects is crucial. Through these practices, the meditator becomes fully absorbed in suchness, like water being poured into water, free of every stain of duality. At the first moment when the practitioner gains direct insight into emptiness, he or she attains the path of seeing. Since these realizations are gained in conjunction with the awakening mind, it is obvious we are talking about the Mahayana path. Of the ten Bodhisattva levels, the meditator attains the first, known as the joyful. This path has two segments—uninterrupted and liberated. During the former path, the obstruction with respect to this realization is counteracted, and having overcome that obstacle, the path of liberation is attained.

With sustained meditation, the practitioner eliminates the obstructions and attains the path of meditation. During the last moment of the concentration known as the vajra-like path of meditation, the subtlest obscurities are eliminated from their very root. Thus, the individual generates the omniscient transcendent wisdom and transforms into a Buddha.

> **In this way, a person who has entered the first level, later, in the path of meditation, familiarizes himself with the two wisdoms of the transcendental state and the subsequent wisdom and skillful means. In this way he gradually purifies the subtlest accumulation of obscurations that are the object of purification of the path of meditation. And in order to achieve higher**

qualities he thoroughly purifies the lower spiritual levels. All purposes and objectives are completely fulfilled by entering the transcendental wisdom of the Tathagatas and by entering the ocean of omniscience. In this way, by gradual practice, the mindstream is thoroughly purified. The *Descent into Lanka* explains this. The *Unraveling of the Thought* too reads, "In order to achieve those higher levels, the mind should be purified just as you refine gold, until you realize the unsurpassable and perfectly consummated Buddhahood."

Entering the ocean of omniscience, you possess impeccable jewel-like qualities to sustain sentient beings, and these fulfill your previous positive prayers. The individual then becomes the embodiment of compassion, possessing various skillful means that function spontaneously and work in various emanations in the interest of all wandering beings. In addition, all marvelous attributes are perfected. With total elimination of all defilements and their latent potential, all Buddhas abide to help every sentient being. Through such realization, generate faith in the Buddhas, the source of all wonderful knowledge and qualities. Everyone should endeavor to actualize these qualities.

The Buddha thus said, "The omniscient transcendental wisdom is produced with compassion as its root, the awakening mind of bodhichitta as its cause, and is perfected by skillful means."

To summarize the teachings of this precious text, we realize that first the two truths must be established, because they are the basis. In the course of practice, the two types of accumulations and the method and wisdom aspects of the path should be implemented in perfect harmony. Two types of Buddha-bodies are achieved as the result. When an individual attains the omniscient state of Buddhahood, all disturbing emotions and obscurations are eliminated once and for all. The person thus awakens to full knowledge. From there onwards, such an awakened being has unlimited potential in helping sentient beings to achieve freedom and liberation.

> **The wise distance themselves from jealousy and**
> **other stains;**
> **Their thirst for knowledge is unquenchable**
> **Like an ocean.**
> **They retain only what is proper through discrimination,**
> **Just like swans extracting milk from water.**
>
> **Thus, scholars should distance themselves**
> **From divisive attitudes and bigotry.**
> **Even from a child**
> **Good words are received.**
>
> **Whatever merit I derive**
> **From the exposition of this Middle Path,**
> **I dedicate for all beings**
> **To actualize the Middle Path.**
>
> **The Second Part of the Stages of Meditation by Acharya Kamalashila is here completed. Translated and edited in Tibetan by the Indian abbot Prajna Verma and the monk Yeshe De.**

We have now finished the teaching of this beautiful text by the great Kamalashila. The author and his master Shantarakshita had a special karmic relationship with the people of the Land of

Snow, and their kindness was beyond estimation. I am happy that I have been able to give this explanatory transmission of the Second Part of Kamalashila's *Stages of Meditation.* I urge all of you listening to or reading this to study the text. To further enhance and extend your understanding of the Middle Way, you should also study the excellent texts on Madhyamika by Buddhapalita and Chandrakirti, who propounded the ultimate viewpoint of the Madhyamika School of thought.

Glossary

awakening mind of bodhichitta: An altruistic wish to achieve Buddhahood for the sake of all sentient beings.

calm abiding: A term which theoretically includes all types of meditative stabilization and refers to a single-pointed state of concentration.

cause of equal state: A cause which producces and develops results similar to itself, e.g. producing barley from barley, or a virtuous action from a virtuous action (one of the six causes).

causes and conditions: Cause produces the nature/entity and the condition produces the characteristics.

commitment being: A meditational deity imagined or visualized in front of yourself.

concomitant cause: A type of cause which contributes toward the production of the fruit through its concomitant presence, e.g. the mind and mental factors arise together by mutually assisting each other (one of the six causes).

direct cause: A cause that produces its result directly without having the need to go through another medium; e.g., fire producing smoke.

distraction: Any kind of mental distraction due to attachment or something else.

eighteen elements: Six external elements or elements of focus (form, sound, smell, taste, contact, and Dharma/object), six internal elements or elements of the basis (eye, ear, nose, tongue, body, and mind), and six elements of the consciousness or dependent elements (eye consciousness, ear consciousness, nose consciousness, tongue consciousness, body consciousness, and mental consciousness).

emptiness: This refers to the lack of independent or absolute existence and is not equal to nothingness or non-existence.

excitement: When the mind is distracted due to attachment.

five mental and physical aggregates: Form, feeling, discrimination, action, and consciousness.

four schools of philosophical tenets: Vaibhashika, Sautrantika, Chittamatra, and Madhyamika.

four truths: True suffering, true cause, true cessation, and true path.

immediate condition: This refers to the immediate production of subsequent mind and mental factors by the concomitant mind and mental factors as soon as the preceding ones cease (one of the four factors/conditions).

indirect cause: A cause which produces its results through the medium of other factors or objects.

mental dullness: This is a mind that lacks clarity, whether focused on a virtuous, non-virtuous, or neutral object.

method and wisdom: Method refers to practices like the development of the awakening mind of bodhichitta; wisdom refers to practices leading to the wisdom realizing emptiness.

non-abiding nirvana: Nirvana at the level of Buddhahood. This is called non-abiding as the Buddha does not abide in either of the two extremes of the cycle of existence or the one-sided peace of nirvana for his own benefit.

objective condition: A condition that produces a consciousness in the aspect of the object, like the arising of a consciousness observing external objects like form, sound, etc. (one of the four factors/conditions).

pliancy: Pliancy is one of the eleven virtuous mental factors that render the body and mind serviceable for virtuous activities and eliminate obstructive and negative states of mind.

renunciation: Common rendering of a term that refers to the determination to be free from the prison-like three realms of existence and to transcend suffering. Thus, it is a wish to become liberated from all states of being within the cycle of existence.

seven branch practices: Practices of prostration, offering, confession, rejoicing, requesting the Buddhas to turn the wheel of Dharma, requesting the Buddhas not to pass away, and dedication.

six states of existence: Hells, hungry ghosts, animals, human beings, demi-gods, and gods.

special insight: A special wisdom which sees the ultimate nature of phenomena.

substantial cause: A cause that primarily produces its result as its substantial continuity; e.g., production of a sprout from a seed.

Tathagata: One Gone Thus—an epithet of the Buddha that refers to one who, by pursuing the path of thusness of emptiness, which is free from the extremes of the cycle of existence and the peace of nirvana, has reached the state of great enlightenment.

ten powers: The power of knowing what is proper and improper; the power of knowing the result of an action; the power of knowing various dispositions; the power of knowing various interests; the power of knowing superior and inferior mental faculties; the power of knowing the path that leads to all; the power of knowing concentrations, liberations, meditative stabilizations, and absorptions, etc.; the power of recollecting past and future lives; the power of knowing death and birth; and the power of knowing the cessation of contamination.

torpor: One of the twenty secondary afflictive emotions; a mind which is distracted toward the object out of attachment or hatred and does not abide within.

twelve sources: The twelve sources are like causes, or doors, for the arising and development of the six consciousnesses (the eye consciousness, etc.). Thus there are six internal sources: eye, ear, nose, tongue, body, and mind, and six external sources: form, sound, smell, taste, contact, and object or phenomenon.

two truths: Conventional truth and ultimate truth.

wisdom being: When a meditational deity is visualized in front of oneself, the wisdom being refers to the actual deity that is imagined to enter into it.

Bibliography of Works Cited

Sutras

Bodhisattva Section Sutra
Bodhisattvapiṭakasūtra
Byang-chub-sems-dpa'i-sde-snod-kyi-mdo

Chapter on Controlling Evil Forces Sutra
Māradamanaparichchhedasūtra
bDud-btul-ba'i-le'u

Cloud of Jewels Sutra
Ratnameghasūtra
dKon-mchog-sprin-gyi-mdo

Compendium of Perfect Dharma Sutra
Dharmasaṃgītisūtra
Chos-yang-dag-par-sdud-pa'i-mdo

Descent into Lanka Sutra
Laṅkāvatārasūtra
Lang-kar-gshegs-pa'i-mdo

Extensive Collection of All Qualities Sutra
Sarvadharmasaṃgrahavaipulyasūtra
Chos-thams-chad-shin-tu-rgyas-pa-bsdus-pa'i-mdo

First Among the Supreme and Glorious
Shrīparamādya
dPal-mchog-dang-po

Heap of Jewels Sutra
Mahāratnakūṭadharmaparyāyashatasāhasrikagranthasūtra
dKon-mchog-brtsegs-pa-chen-po'i-chos-kyi-rnam-grangs-le'u-stong-phrag-brgya-pa'i-mdo

Hill of the Gaya Head Sutra
Gayāshīrṣhasūtra
Ga-ya-mgo'i-ri'i-mdo

Jewel in the Crown Sutra
Ratnachūḍasūtra
gTsug-na-rin-po-che'i-mdo

King of Meditative Stabilization Sutra
Samādhirājasūtra
Ting-nge-'dzin-rgyal-po'i-mdo

Meditation on Faith in the Mahayana Sutra
Mahāyānaprasādaprabhāvanāsūtra
Theg-pa-chen-po-la-dad-pa-sgom-pa'i-mdo

Moon Lamp Sutra
Chandrapradīpasūtra
Zla-ba-sgron-me'i-mdo

Prayer of Noble Conduct
Bhadracharī
bZang-po-spyod-pa'i-smon-lam

Perfection of Wisdom Sutra
Prajñāpāramitāsūtra
Shes-rab-kyi-pha-rol-tu-phyin-pa'i-mdo

Pure Field of Engagement Sutra
Gocharaparishuddhasūtra
sPyod-yul-yongs-su-dag-pa'i-l'eu

Questions of Narayana
Nārāyāṇaparipṛchchhasūtra
Sred-med-kyi-bus-zhus-pa

Sutra on the Elimination of Ajatashatru's Regret
Ajātashatrukaukṛtyavinodanasūtra
Ma-skyes-dgra'i-'gyod-pa-bsal-ba'i-mdo

Sutra of the Great and Complete Transcendence of Suffering
Mahāparinirvāṇasūtra
Yongs-su-mya-ngan-las-'das-pa-chen-po'i-mdo

Space Treasure Sutra
Gaganagañjasūtra
Nam-mkha'-mdzod

Teaching of Vimalakirti Sutra
Vimalakīrtinirdeshasūtra
Dri-ma-med-par-grags-pas-bstan-pa

Teaching of Akshayamati Sutra
Akṣhayamatinirdeshasūtra
Blo-gros-mi-zad-pas-bstan-pa'i-mdo

Ten Spiritual Levels Sutra
Dashabhūmikasūtra
mDo sde sa bcu pa

Ten Qualities Sutra
Dashadharmakasūtra
Chos-bcu-pa'i-mdo

Unraveling of the Thought Sutra
Saṃdhinirmochanasūtra
dGongs-pa-nges-par-'grel-pa'i-mdo

Treatises

Commentary on (Dignaga's) "Compendium of Valid Cognition"
Pramāṇavarttikakārikā
Tshad-ma-rnam-'grel-gyi-tshig-le'ur-byas-pa
by Dharmakīrti

Compendium of Knowledge
Abhidharmasamuchchaya
mNgon-pa-kun-btus
by Asaṅga

Guide to the Bodhisattva's Way of Life
Bodhisattvacharyāvatāra
Byang-chub-sems-dpa'i-spyod-pa-la-'jug-pa
by Shāntideva

Essence of Madhyamaka
Madhyamakahṛdayakārikā
dBu-ma-snying-po'i-tshig-le'ur-byas-pa
by Bhāvaviveka

Illumination of the Middle Way
Madhyamakāloka
dBu-ma-snang-ba
by Kamalashīla

Nagarjuna's Fundamental Treatise on the Middle Way, called "Wisdom"
Prajñānāmamūlamadhyamakakārikā
dBu-ma-rtsa-ba'i-tshig-le'ur-byas-pa-shes-rab-ces-bya-ba
by Nāgārjuna

Tibetan Text of The Stages of Meditation II

by Kamalashila

༄༅། །བསྒོམ་རིམ་བར་པ།

༄༅། །རྒྱ་གར་སྐད་དུ། བྷཱཝནཱཀྲམ། བོད་སྐད་དུ། བསྒོམ་པའི་རིམ་པ། འཇམ་དཔལ་གཞོན་ནུར་གྱུར་པ་ལ་ཕྱག་འཚལ་ལོ།

ཐེག་པ་ཆེན་པོའི་མདོ་སྡེའི་ཚུལ་གྱི་རྗེས་སུ་འཇུག་པ་རྣམས་ཀྱི་བསྒོམ་པའི་རིམ་པ་མདོར་བཤད་དོ། འདི་ལ་ཐམས་ཅད་མཁྱེན་པ་ཉིད་ཤིན་ཏུ་མྱུར་དུ་ཐོབ་པར་འདོད་པ་རྟོག་པ་དང་ལྡན་པས་དེ་ཐོབ་པར་བྱེད་པའི་རྒྱུ་རྣམས་དང་རྐྱེན་རྣམས་ལ་མངོན་པར་བརྩོན་པར་བྱའོ།

འདི་ལྟར་ཐམས་ཅད་མཁྱེན་པ་ཉིད་འདི་ནི་རྒྱུ་མེད་པ་ལས་འབྱུང་བར་མི་རུང་སྟེ། ཐམས་ཅད་ཀྱང་དུས་ཐམས་ཅད་དུ་ཐམས་ཅད་མཁྱེན་པ་ཉིད་དུ་འབྱུང་བར་ཐལ་བར་གྱུར་པའི་ཕྱིར་རོ། ལྟོས་པ་མེད་པར་འབྱུང་ན་ནི་གང་དུ་ཡང་ཐོགས་པར་མི་རུང་སྟེ། གང་གིས་ན་ཐམས་ཅད་ཀྱང་ཐམས་ཅད་མཁྱེན་པ་ཉིད་དུ་མི་འགྱུར་རོ། དེ་ལྟ་བས་ན་ལ་ལར་བརྒྱ་ལམ་ན་འགའ་ཞིག་འབྱུང་དུ་ཟད་པས་དངོས་པོ་ཐམས་ཅད་ནི་རྒྱུ་ལ་ལྟོས་པ་ཁོ་ན་ཡིན་ནོ། ཐམས་ཅད་མཁྱེན་པ་ཉིད་དུ་ཡང་ལ་ལར་བརྒྱ་ལམ་ན་འགའ་ཞིག་འགྱུར་ཏེ། དུས་ཐམས་ཅད་དུ་མ་ཡིན། གནས་ཐམས་ཅད་དུ་ཡང་མ་ཡིན། ཐམས་ཅད་ཀྱང་མ་ཡིན་པས་དེའི་ཕྱིར་དེ་ནི་རྒྱུ་དང་རྐྱེན་ལ་ལྟོས་པར་ངེས་སོ། རྒྱུ་དང་རྐྱེན་དེ་དག་གི་ནང་ནས་ཀྱང་མ་ནོར་ཅིང་མ་ཚང་བ་མེད་པ་རྣམས་བསྟེན་པར་བྱའོ། རྒྱུ་ནོར་བ་ལ་ནན་ཏན་བྱས་ན་ནི་ཡུན་

ཤིན་ཏུ་རིང་པོ་ཞིག་གིས་ཀྱང་འདོད་པའི་འབྲས་བུ་འཐོབ་པ་མེད་དོ། དཔེར་ན། རྣ་ལས་འོ་མ་བཞོ་བ་བཞིན་ནོ། རྒྱུ་མཐའ་དག་མ་སྤྱད་པ་ལས་ཀྱང་འབྲས་བུ་འབྱུང་བ་མེད་དེ། ས་བོན་ལ་སོགས་པ་གང་ཡང་རུང་བ་ཞིག་མེད་ན་མྱུ་གུ་ལ་སོགས་པ་འབྲས་བུ་མི་འབྱུང་བའི་ཕྱིར་རོ། དེ་ལྟ་བས་ན་འབྲས་བུ་དེ་འདོད་པས་རྒྱུ་དང་རྐྱེན་མ་ནོར་བ་དང་མཐའ་དག་ལ་བརྟེན་པར་བྱའོ།

འབྲས་བུ་ཐམས་ཅད་མཁྱེན་པ་ཉིད་ཀྱི་རྒྱུ་དང་རྐྱེན་དེ་དག་གང་ཞེ་ན། སྨྲས་པ། བདག་ལྟ་བུ་དམུས་ལོང་དང་འདྲ་བས་དེ་དག་བསྟན་པར་མི་ནུས་མོད་ཀྱི། འོན་ཀྱང་བཅོམ་ལྡན་འདས་ཉིད་ཀྱིས་མངོན་པར་རྫོགས་པར་སངས་རྒྱས་ནས་གདུལ་བྱ་རྣམས་ལ་ཇི་སྐད་བཤད་པ་དེ་བཞིན་དུ་བདག་གིས་བཅོམ་ལྡན་འདས་ཀྱི་བཀའ་ཉིད་ཀྱིས་བཤད་དོ། བཅོམ་ལྡན་འདས་ཀྱིས་དེར་བཀའ་སྩལ་པ། གསང་བའི་བདག་པོ་ཐམས་ཅད་མཁྱེན་པའི་ཡེ་ཤེས་དེ་ནི་སྙིང་རྗེའི་རྩ་བ་ལས་བྱུང་བ་ཡིན། བྱང་ཆུབ་ཀྱི་སེམས་ཀྱི་རྒྱུ་ལས་བྱུང་བ་ཡིན། ཐབས་ཀྱིས་མཐར་ཕྱིན་པ་ཡིན་ནོ། ཞེས་འབྱུང་ངོ་། དེ་ལྟ་བས་ན་ཐམས་ཅད་མཁྱེན་པ་ཉིད་ཐོབ་པར་འདོད་པས་སྙིང་རྗེ་དང་། བྱང་ཆུབ་ཀྱི་སེམས་དང་། ཐབས་དང་གསུམ་པོ་འདི་དག་ལ་བསླབ་པར་བྱའོ།

སྙིང་རྗེས་བསྐྱོད་ན་བྱང་ཆུབ་སེམས་དཔའ་རྣམས་སེམས་ཅན་ཐམས་ཅད་མངོན་པར་གདོན་པའི་ཕྱིར་ངེས་པར་དམ་འཆའ་བར་འགྱུར་རོ། དེ་ནས་བདག་ཉིད་ལ་ལྟ་བ་བསལ་ནས་ཤིན་ཏུ་བྱ་དཀའ་ཞིང་རྒྱུན་མི་ཆད་ལ་ཡུན་རིང་པོར་བསྒྲུབས་པའི་བསོད་ནམས་དང་ཡེ་ཤེས་ཀྱི་ཚོགས་ལ་གུས་

པར་འཇུག་གོ །དེར་ཞུགས་ནས་ངེས་པར་བསོད་ནམས་དང་ཡེ་ཤེས་ཀྱི་ཚོགས་ཡོངས་སུ་རྫོགས་པར་སྒྲུབ་བོ། ཚོགས་རྣམས་ཡོངས་སུ་རྫོགས་ན་ཐམས་ཅད་མཁྱེན་པ་ཉིད་ལག་མཐིལ་དུ་ཐོབ་པ་དང་འདྲ་བར་འགྱུར་རོ། དེ་བས་ན་ཐམས་ཅད་མཁྱེན་པ་ཉིད་ཀྱི་རྩ་བ་ནི་སྙིང་རྗེ་ཁོ་ན་ཡིན་པས་དེ་ནི་ཐོག་མ་ཁོ་ནར་གོམས་པར་བྱའོ།

ཆོས་ཡང་དག་པར་སྡུད་པ་ལས་ཀྱང་བཀའ་སྩལ་ཏེ། བཅོམ་ལྡན་འདས་བྱང་ཆུབ་སེམས་དཔས་ཆོས་རབ་ཏུ་མང་པོ་ལ་བསླབ་པར་མི་བགྱིའོ། བཅོམ་ལྡན་འདས་བྱང་ཆུབ་སེམས་པས་ཆོས་གཅིག་རབ་ཏུ་གཟུང་ཞིང་རབ་ཏུ་རྟོགས་པར་བགྱིས་ན་སངས་རྒྱས་ཀྱི་ཆོས་ཐམས་ཅད་དེའི་ལག་མཐིལ་དུ་མཆིས་པ་ལགས་སོ། ཆོས་གཅིག་པོ་གང་ཞེ་ན། འདི་ལྟ་སྟེ་སྙིང་རྗེ་ཆེན་པོའོ། ཞེས་འབྱུང་ངོ་།

སྙིང་རྗེ་ཆེན་པོས་ཡོངས་སུ་ཟིན་པས་ན་སངས་རྒྱས་བཅོམ་ལྡན་འདས་རྣམས་རང་གི་དོན་ཕུན་སུམ་ཚོགས་པ་མཐའ་དག་བརྙེས་ཀྱང་སེམས་ཅན་གྱི་ཁམས་མཐར་ཐུག་པའི་བར་དུ་བཞུགས་པར་མཛད་དོ། ཉན་ཐོས་བཞིན་དུ་མྱ་ངན་ལས་འདས་པའི་གྲོང་ཁྱེར་ཤིན་ཏུ་ཞི་བར་ཡང་འཇུག་པར་མི་མཛད་དེ། སེམས་ཅན་ལ་གཟིགས་ནས་མྱ་ངན་ལས་འདས་པའི་གྲོང་ཁྱེར་ཞི་བ་དེ་ལྕགས་ཀྱི་ཁང་པ་འབར་བ་བཞིན་དུ་ཐག་རིང་དུ་སྤོང་བས་བཅོམ་ལྡན་འདས་རྣམས་ཀྱི་མི་གནས་པའི་མྱ་ངན་ལས་འདས་པའི་རྒྱུ་ནི་སྙིང་རྗེ་ཆེན་པོ་དེ་ཉིད་ཡིན་ནོ།

དེ་ལ་སྙིང་རྗེ་བསྒོམ་པའི་རིམ་པ་དེ་དང་པོ་འཇུག་པ་ནས་བརྩམས་ཏེ་བརྗོད་པར་བྱའོ། ཐོག་མར་རེ་ཞིག་བཏང་སྙོམས་བསྒོམས་པས་སེམས་ཅན་ཐམས་ཅད་ལ་རྗེས་སུ་ཆགས་པ་དང་། ཁོང་ཁྲོ་བ་བསལ་ཏེ་སྙོམས་པའི་སེམས་ཉིད་བསྒྲུབ་པར་བྱའོ།

སེམས་ཅན་ཐམས་ཅད་བདེ་བ་ནི་འདོད་སྡུག་བསྔལ་བ་ནི་མི་འདོད་ལ། ཐོག་མ་མེད་པ་ཅན་གྱི་འཁོར་བ་ན་སེམས་ཅན་གང་ལན་བརྒྱར་དག་གི་གཉེན་དུ་མ་གྱུར་པ་དེ་གང་ཡང་མེད་དོ་སྙམ་དུ་ཡོངས་སུ་བསམས་ཞིང་། འདི་ལ་བྱེ་བྲག་ཅི་ཞིག་ཡོད་ན་ལ་ལ་ལ་ནི་རྗེས་སུ་ཆགས། ལ་ལ་ལ་ནི་ཁོང་ཁྲོ་བར་གྱུར་བས། དེ་ལྟ་བས་ན་བདག་གིས་སེམས་ཅན་ཐམས་ཅད་ལ་སེམས་སྙོམས་པ་ཉིད་དུ་བྱའོ་སྙམ་དུ་དེ་ལྟར་ཡིད་ལ་བྱ་ཞིང་བར་མའི་ཕྱོགས་ནས་བརྩམས་ཏེ། མཛའ་བཤེས་དང་དགྲ་ལ་ཡང་སེམས་སྙོམས་པ་ཉིད་དུ་བསྒོམ་མོ། དེ་ནས་སེམས་ཅན་ཐམས་ཅད་ལ་སེམས་སྙོམས་པ་ཉིད་དུ་བསྒྲུབས་ནས་བྱམས་པ་བསྒོམ་མོ། བྱམས་པའི་ཆུས་སེམས་ཀྱི་རྒྱུད་བརླན་ཏེ་སེར་ཡོད་པའི་ས་གཞི་བཞིན་དུ་བྱས་ལ་སྙིང་རྗེའི་ས་བོན་བཏབ་ན་བདེ་བླག་ཏུ་ཤིན་ཏུ་ཡོངས་སུ་རྒྱས་པར་འགྱུར་རོ། དེ་ནས་སེམས་ཀྱི་རྒྱུད་བྱམས་པས་བསྒོས་ནས་སྙིང་རྗེ་བསྒོམ་པར་བྱའོ།

སྙིང་རྗེ་དེ་ནི་སེམས་ཅན་སྡུག་བསྔལ་བ་ཐམས་ཅད་སྡུག་བསྔལ་དེ་དང་བྲལ་བར་འདོད་པའི་རྣམ་པ་ཡིན་ན། ཁམས་གསུམ་པའི་སེམས་ཅན་ཐམས་ཅད་ནི་སྡུག་བསྔལ་ཉིད་རྣམ་པ་གསུམ་གྱིས་ཅི་རིགས་པར་ཤིན་ཏུ

སྡུག་བསྔལ་བ་དག་ཡིན་པས་དེའི་ཕྱིར་སེམས་ཅན་ཐམས་ཅད་ལ་དེ་བསྒོམ་པར་བྱ་སྟེ། འདི་ལྟར་རེ་ཞིག་སེམས་ཅན་དམྱལ་བ་པའི་སེམས་ཅན་གང་དག་ཡིན་པ་དེ་དག་ནི་རྒྱུན་མི་ཆད་ཅིང་ཡུན་རིང་ལ་ཚ་བ་ལ་སོགས་པའི་སྡུག་བསྔལ་སྣ་ཚོགས་ཀྱི་ཆུ་བོར་བྱིང་བ་ཁོ་ན་ཡིན་ནོ། ཞེས་བཅོམ་ལྡན་འདས་ཀྱིས་བཀའ་སྩལ་ཏོ། དེ་བཞིན་དུ་ཡི་དྭགས་རྣམས་ཀྱང་ཕལ་ཆེར་ཤིན་ཏུ་མི་བཟད་པའི་བཀྲེས་པ་དང་སྐོམ་པའི་སྡུག་བསྔལ་གྱི་མེས་བསྐམས་པའི་ལུས་ཤིན་ཏུ་སྡུག་བསྔལ་མང་པོ་མྱོང་ངོ་། ཞེས་བཀའ་སྩལ་ཏོ། དུད་འགྲོ་རྣམས་ཀྱང་གཅིག་ལ་གཅིག་ཟ་བ་དང་། ཁྲོ་བ་དང་། གསོད་པ་དང་། རྣམ་པར་འཚེ་བ་ལ་སོགས་པའི་སྡུག་བསྔལ་རྣམ་པ་མང་པོ་མྱོང་བ་ཁོ་ནར་སྣང་ངོ་། མི་རྣམས་ཀྱང་འདོད་པ་ཡོངས་སུ་ཚོལ་བས་ཕོངས་ནས་གཅིག་ལ་གཅིག་འཁྲུ་བ་དང་། གནོད་པ་བྱེད་པ་དང་། སྡུག་པ་དང་བྲལ་བ་དང་། མི་སྡུག་པ་དང་ཕྲད་པ་དང་། དབུལ་ཕོངས་ལས་གྱུར་པ་ལ་སོགས་པའི་སྡུག་བསྔལ་དཔག་ཏུ་མེད་པ་ཉམས་སུ་མྱོང་བར་སྣང་ངོ་།

གང་དག་འདོད་ཆགས་ལ་སོགས་པའི་ཉོན་མོངས་པས་ཀུན་ནས་དཀྲིས་པ་སྣ་ཚོགས་ཀྱིས་སེམས་དཀྲིས་པ་དག་དང་། གང་དག་ལྟ་བ་ངན་པ་རྣམ་པ་སྣ་ཚོགས་གཟིང་གཟིང་བར་གྱུར་པ་དེ་ཐམས་ཅད་ཀྱང་སྡུག་བསྔལ་གྱི་རྒྱུ་ཡིན་པས་གད་ཀ་ན་འདུག་པ་བཞིན་དུ་ཤིན་ཏུ་སྡུག་བསྔལ་བ་ཁོ་ན་ཡིན་ནོ། ལྷ་རྣམས་ཀྱང་ཐམས་ཅད་འགྱུར་བའི་སྡུག་བསྔལ་ཉིད་ཀྱིས་སྡུག་བསྔལ་བ་དག་སྟེ། འདོད་པ་ན་སྤྱོད་པའི་ལྷ་གང་དག་ཡིན་པ་དེ་དག་ནི་རྟག་ཏུ་

འཆི་འཕོ་བ་དང་ལྟུང་བ་ལ་སོགས་པའི་འཇིགས་པའི་མྱ་ངན་གྱིས་སེམས་ལ་གནོན་ན་ཇི་ལྟར་བདེ། འདུ་བྱེད་ཀྱི་སྡུག་བསྔལ་ཉིད་ནི་ལས་དང་ཉོན་མོངས་པའི་མཚན་ཉིད་ཀྱི་རྒྱུའི་གཞན་གྱི་དབང་གི་ངོ་བོ་ཉིད་དང་། སྐད་ཅིག་རེ་རེ་ལ་འཇིག་པའི་ངང་ཅན་གྱི་མཚན་ཉིད་དེ། འགྲོ་བ་ཐམས་ཅད་ལ་ཁྱབ་པ་ཡིན་ནོ། དེ་བས་ན་འགྲོ་བ་མཐའ་དག་ནི་སྡུག་བསྔལ་གྱི་མེ་ལྕེ་འབར་བའི་ནང་དུ་ཞུགས་པ་ཡིན་པར་བལྟས་ལ་ཇི་ལྟར་སྡུག་བསྔལ་མི་འདོད་པ་ལྟར་གཞན་ཐམས་ཅད་ཀྱང་དེ་དང་འདྲའོ་སྙམ་དུ་བསམ་ཞིང་། ཀྱི་མ་ཀྱི་ཧུད་བདག་ལ་སྡུག་པའི་སེམས་ཅན་འདི་དག་སྡུག་བསྔལ་ན། སྡུག་བསྔལ་དེ་ལས་ཇི་ལྟར་ཐར་བར་བྱ་ཞེས་བདག་ཉིད་སྡུག་བསྔལ་བ་བཞིན་དུ་བྱེད་ཅིང་དེ་དང་བྲལ་བར་འདོད་པའི་རྣམ་པའི་སྙིང་རྗེ་དེས་ཏིང་ངེ་འཛིན་ལ་འདུག་ཀྱང་རུང་། སྤྱོད་ལམ་ཐམས་ཅད་དུ་ཡང་རུང་སྟེ། དུས་ཐམས་ཅད་དུ་སེམས་ཅན་ཐམས་ཅད་ལ་བསྒོམ་པར་བྱ་སྟེ། ཐོག་མ་ཁོ་ནར་མཛའ་བཤེས་ཀྱི་ཕྱོགས་རྣམས་ལ་ཇི་སྐད་སྨོས་པའི་སྡུག་བསྔལ་སྣ་ཚོགས་ཉམས་སུ་མྱོང་བར་མཐོང་བས་བསྒོམ་པར་བྱའོ།

དེ་ནས་སེམས་ཅན་མཉམ་པ་ཉིད་ཀྱིས་བྱེ་བྲག་མེད་པར་མཐོང་ནས་སེམས་ཅན་ཐམས་ཅད་ནི་བདག་གི་གཉེན་དུ་གྱུར་པ་ཁོ་ནའོ་སྙམ་དུ་ཡོངས་སུ་བསམ་ཞིང་བར་མའི་ཕྱོགས་རྣམས་ལ་བསྒོམ་པར་བྱའོ། གང་གི་ཚེ་དེ་ལ་མཛའ་བཤེས་ཀྱི་ཕྱོགས་བཞིན་དུ་སྙིང་རྗེ་དེ་མཉམ་པར་ཞུགས་པར་གྱུར་པ་དེའི་ཚེ་ཕྱོགས་བཅུའི་སེམས་ཅན་ཐམས་ཅད་ལ་བསྒོམ་པར་བྱའོ། གང་

གི་ཚེ་བུ་ཆུང་ངུ་སྙིང་དུ་སྡུག་པ་སྡུག་བསྔལ་བར་གྱུར་པའི་མ་བཞིན་དུ་བདག་ཉིད་ཀྱིས་ཤིན་ཏུ་སྡུག་པ་སྡུག་བསྔལ་བ་ལས་འདོན་པར་འདོད་པའི་རྣམ་པ་རང་གི་ངང་གིས་འཇུག་པའི་སྙིང་རྗེ་དེ་སེམས་ཅན་ཐམས་ཅད་ལ་མཉམ་པར་ཞུགས་པར་གྱུར་པ་དེའི་ཚེ་རྫོགས་པ་ཞེས་བྱ་སྟེ། སྙིང་རྗེ་ཆེན་པོའི་མིང་ཡང་འཐོབ་བོ།

བྱམས་པ་བསྒོམ་པ་ནི་མཛའ་བཤེས་ཀྱི་ཕྱོགས་ལ་ཐོག་མར་བྱས་ནས་བདེ་བ་དང་ཕྲད་པར་འདོད་པའི་རྣམ་པ་སྟེ། རིམ་གྱིས་ཐ་མལ་པ་དང་དགྲ་ལ་ཡང་བསྒོམ་པར་བྱའོ། དེ་ལྟར་དེ་སྙིང་རྗེ་གོམས་པར་བྱས་ནས། རིམ་གྱིས་སེམས་ཅན་མཐའ་དག་མངོན་པར་འདོན་པར་འདོད་པ་རང་གི་ངང་གིས་འབྱུང་བ་ཉིད་དུ་འགྱུར་རོ།

དེས་ན་ཙ་བའི་སྙིང་རྗེ་གོམས་པར་བྱས་ནས་བྱང་ཆུབ་ཀྱི་སེམས་བསྒོམ་པར་བྱའོ། བྱང་ཆུབ་ཀྱི་སེམས་དེ་ནི་རྣམ་པ་གཉིས་ཏེ། ཀུན་རྫོབ་དང་། དོན་དམ་པའོ། དེ་ལ་ཀུན་རྫོབ་པ་ནི་སྙིང་རྗེས་སེམས་ཅན་མཐའ་དག་མངོན་པར་འདོན་པར་དམ་བཅས་ནས་འགྲོ་བ་ལ་ཕན་གདགས་པའི་ཕྱིར་སངས་རྒྱས་སུ་གྱུར་ཅིག་སྙམ་དུ་བླ་ན་མེད་པ་ཡང་དག་པར་རྫོགས་པའི་བྱང་ཆུབ་འདོད་པའི་རྣམ་པས་སེམས་དང་པོ་བསྐྱེད་པའོ། དེ་ཡང་ཚུལ་ཁྲིམས་ཀྱི་ལེའུ་ལས་བསྟན་པའི་ཚོ་ག་བཞིན་དུ་བྱང་ཆུབ་སེམས་དཔའི་སྡོམ་པ་ལ་གནས་པ་མཁས་པ་པ་ཕ་རོལ་པོ་ལས་སེམས་བསྐྱེད་པར་བྱའོ།

དེ་ལྟར་ཀུན་རྫོབ་པའི་བྱང་ཆུབ་ཀྱི་སེམས་བསྐྱེད་ནས་དོན་དམ་པའི

བྱང་ཆུབ་ཀྱི་སེམས་བསྐྱེད་པའི་ཕྱིར་འབད་པར་བྱའོ། དོན་དམ་པའི་བྱང་ཆུབ་ཀྱི་སེམས་དེ་ནི་འཇིག་རྟེན་ལས་འདས་པ་སྤྲོས་པ་མཐའ་དག་དང་བྲལ་བ། ཤིན་ཏུ་གསལ་བ། དོན་དམ་པའི་སྤྱོད་ཡུལ། དྲི་མ་མེད་པ། མི་གཡོ་བ། རླུང་མེད་པའི་མར་མེའི་རྒྱུན་ལྟར་མི་གཡོ་བའོ། དེ་འགྲུབ་པ་ནི་རྟག་ཏུ་གུས་པར་ཡུན་རིང་དུ་ཞི་གནས་དང་ལྷག་མཐོང་གི་རྣལ་འབྱོར་གོམས་པར་བྱས་པ་ལས་འགྱུར་ཏེ། འཕགས་པ་དགོངས་པ་ངེས་པར་འགྲེལ་པ་ལས། ཇི་སྐད་དུ། བྱམས་པ་གང་ཡང་ཉན་ཐོས་རྣམས་ཀྱིའམ། བྱང་ཆུབ་སེམས་དཔའ་རྣམས་ཀྱིའམ། དེ་བཞིན་གཤེགས་པ་རྣམས་ཀྱི་དགེ་བའི་ཆོས་འཇིག་རྟེན་པ་དང་འཇིག་རྟེན་ལས་འདས་པ་ཐམས་ཅད་ཀྱང་ཞི་གནས་དང་ལྷག་མཐོང་གི་འབྲས་བུ་ཡིན་པར་རིག་པར་བྱའོ། ཞེས་གསུངས་པ་ལྟ་བུའོ། དེ་གཉིས་ཀྱིས་ཏིང་ངེ་འཛིན་ཐམས་ཅད་བསྡུས་པའི་ཕྱིར་རྣལ་འབྱོར་པ་ཐམས་ཅད་ཀྱིས་དུས་ཐམས་ཅད་དུ་ངེས་པར་ཞི་གནས་དང་ལྷག་མཐོང་བསྟེན་པར་བྱ་སྟེ། འཕགས་པ་དགོངས་པ་ངེས་པར་འགྲེལ་པ་དེ་ཉིད་ལས། བཅོམ་ལྡན་འདས་ཀྱིས་ཇི་སྐད་དུ་ངས་ཉན་ཐོས་རྣམས་དང་། བྱང་ཆུབ་སེམས་དཔའ་རྣམས་དང་། དེ་བཞིན་གཤེགས་པ་རྣམས་ཀྱི་ཏིང་ངེ་འཛིན་རྣམ་པ་དུ་མ་བསྟན་པ་གང་དག་ཡིན་པ་དེ་དག་ཐམས་ཅད་ཞི་གནས་དང་ལྷག་མཐོང་གིས་བསྡུས་པར་རིག་པར་བྱའོ། ཞེས་གསུངས་པ་ལྟ་བུའོ།

ཞི་གནས་ཙམ་འབའ་ཞིག་གོམས་པར་བྱས་པས་ནི་རྣལ་འབྱོར་རྣམས་ཀྱི་སྒྲིབ་པ་མི་སྤོང་གི །རེ་ཞིག་ཉོན་མོངས་པ་རྣམ་པར་གནོན་པ་ཙམ་དུ་

ཟད་དེ། ཤེས་རབ་ཀྱི་སྣང་བ་བྱུང་བ་མེད་པར་བག་ལ་ཉལ་ལེགས་པར་ཆོམས་མི་སྲིད་པའི་ཕྱིར་བག་ལ་ཉལ་ལེགས་པར་ཆོམས་པར་མི་འགྱུར་རོ། དེ་བས་ན་འཕགས་པ་དགོངས་པ་ངེས་པར་འགྲེལ་པ་དེ་ཉིད་ལས། བསམ་གཏན་གྱིས་ནི་ཉོན་མོངས་པ་རྣམས་རྣམ་པར་གནོན་ཏོ། ཤེས་རབ་ཀྱིས་ནི་བག་ལ་ཉལ་ལེགས་པར་འཇོམས་པར་བྱེད་དོ། ཞེས་བཀའ་བསྩལ་ཏོ། འཕགས་པ་ཏིང་ངེ་འཛིན་རྒྱལ་པོ་ལས་ཀྱང་། ཏིང་ངེ་འཛིན་དེ་སྒོམ་པར་བྱེད་མོད་ཀྱི། །དེ་ནི་བདག་ཏུ་འདུ་ཤེས་འཇིག་མི་བྱེད། །དེ་ནི་ཉོན་མོངས་ཕྱིར་ཞིང་རབ་ཏུ་འཁྲུགས། །ལྷག་སྤྱོད་འདི་ན་ཏིང་འཛིན་བསྒོམ་པ་བཞིན། །གལ་ཏེ་ཆོས་ལ་བདག་མེད་སོ་སོར་རྟོག །སོ་སོར་དེ་བརྟགས་གལ་ཏེ་བསྒོམ་པ་ནི། །དེ་ཉིད་མྱ་ངན་འདས་ཐོབ་འབྲས་བུའི་རྒྱུ། །རྒྱུ་གཞན་གང་ཡིན་དེས་ནི་ཞི་མི་འགྱུར། ཞེས་གསུངས་སོ། བྱང་ཆུབ་སེམས་པའི་སྡེ་སྣོད་ལས་ཀྱང་། གང་དག་བྱང་ཆུབ་སེམས་དཔའི་སྡེ་སྣོད་ཀྱི་ཆོས་ཀྱི་རྣམ་གྲངས་འདི་མ་ཐོས། འཕགས་པའི་ཆོས་འདུལ་བ་མ་ཐོས་པར་ཏིང་ངེ་འཛིན་ཙམ་གྱིས་ཆོག་པར་འཛིན་པ་ནི་ང་རྒྱལ་གྱི་དབང་གིས་མངོན་པའི་ང་རྒྱལ་དུ་ལྷུང་ཞིང་། སྐྱེ་བ་དང་། རྒ་བ་དང་། ན་བ་དང་། འཆི་བ་དང་། མྱ་ངན་དང་། སྨྲེ་སྔགས་འདོན་པ་དང་། སྡུག་བསྔལ་བ་དང་། ཡིད་མི་བདེ་བ་དང་། འཁྲུག་པ་ལས་ཡོངས་སུ་མི་གྲོལ། འགྲོ་བ་དྲུག་གི་འཁོར་བ་ལས་ཡོངས་སུ་མི་གྲོལ། སྡུག་བསྔལ་གྱི་ཕུང་པོ་ལས་ཀྱང་ཡོངས་སུ་མི་གྲོལ་ཏེ། དེ་ལ་དགོངས་ནས་དེ་བཞིན་གཤེགས་པས་འདི་སྐད་ཅེས། གཞན་ལས་རྗེས་སུ་མཐུན་པ་ཐོས་

པ་ནི་ཏ་ཤེ་ལས་གྲོལ་བར་འགྱུར་རོ། ཞེས་བཀའ་བསྩལ་ཏོ། ཞེས་གསུངས་སོ།

དེ་ལྟ་བས་ན་སྒྲིབ་པ་མཐའ་དག་སྤངས་ནས་ཡོངས་སུ་དག་པའི་ཡེ་ཤེས་འབྱུང་བར་འདོད་པས་ཞི་གནས་ལ་གནས་ཤིང་ཤེས་རབ་སྒོམ་པར་བྱའོ། དེ་སྐད་དུ། འཕགས་པ་དཀོན་མཆོག་བརྩེགས་པ་ལས་ཀྱང་བཀའ་སྩལ་ཏེ།

ཚུལ་ཁྲིམས་ལ་ནི་གནས་ནས་ཏིང་ངེ་འཛིན་ཐོབ་སྟེ། ཏིང་ངེ་འཛིན་ཐོབ་ནས་ཀྱང་ཤེས་རབ་སྒོམ་པར་བྱེད། ཤེས་རབ་ཀྱིས་ནི་ཡེ་ཤེས་རྣམ་པར་དག་པ་འཐོབ། ཡེ་ཤེས་རྣམ་པར་དག་པས་ཚུལ་ཁྲིམས་ཕུན་སུམ་ཚོགས། ཞེས་བཀའ་བསྩལ་ཏོ།

འཕགས་པ་ཐེག་པ་ཆེན་པོ་ལ་དད་པ་བསྒོམ་པའི་མདོ་ལས་ཀྱང་། རིགས་ཀྱི་བུ་ཤེས་རབ་ལ་ཉེ་བར་མི་གནས་ན་བྱང་ཆུབ་སེམས་དཔའ་རྣམས་ཀྱིས་ཐེག་པ་ཆེན་པོ་ལ་དད་པ་ཐེག་པ་ཆེན་པོ་ལ་ཇི་ལྟར་ཡང་འབྱུང་བར་ང་མི་སྨྲའོ། རིགས་ཀྱི་བུ་རྣམ་གྲངས་འདིས་ཀྱང་འདི་ལྟར་བྱང་ཆུབ་སེམས་དཔའ་རྣམས་ཀྱི་ཐེག་པ་ཆེན་པོ་ལ་དད་པ་ཐེག་པ་ཆེན་པོ་ལ་འབྱུང་བ་གང་ཅི་ཡང་རུང་། དེ་ཐམས་ཅད་ནི་རྣམ་པར་མི་གཡེངས་པའི་སེམས་ཀྱིས་དོན་དང་ཆོས་ཡང་དག་པར་བསམས་པ་ལས་བྱུང་བར་རིག་པར་བྱའོ། ཞེས་བཀའ་བསྩལ་ཏོ།

ཞི་གནས་དང་བྲལ་བའི་ལྷག་མཐོང་འབའ་ཞིག་གིས་ནི་རྣལ་འབྱོར་པའི་སེམས་ཡུལ་རྣམས་ལ་རྣམ་པར་གཡེང་བར་འགྱུར་གྱི། རླུང་གི་ནང་

ན་འདུག་པའི་མར་མེ་བཞིན་དུ་བརྟན་པར་མི་འགྱུར་རོ། དེ་བས་ན་ཡེ་ཤེས་ཀྱི་སྣང་བ་ཤིན་ཏུ་གསལ་བར་མི་འབྱུང་སྟེ། དེ་ལྟ་བས་ན་གཉིས་ཀ་དང་འདྲ་བར་བསྟེན་པར་བྱའོ། དེའི་ཕྱིར་འཕགས་པ་ཡོངས་སུ་མྱ་ངན་ལས་འདས་པ་ཆེན་པོའི་མདོ་ལས་ཀྱང་། ཉན་ཐོས་རྣམས་ཀྱིས་ནི་དེ་བཞིན་གཤེགས་པའི་རིགས་མི་མཐོང་སྟེ། ཏིང་ངེ་འཛིན་གྱི་ཤས་ཆེ་བའི་ཕྱིར་དང་། ཤེས་རབ་ཆུང་བའི་ཕྱིར་རོ། བྱང་ཆུབ་སེམས་དཔའ་རྣམས་ཀྱིས་ནི་མཐོང་མོད་ཀྱི་མི་གསལ་ཏེ། ཤེས་རབ་ཀྱི་ཤས་ཆེ་བའི་ཕྱིར་དང་། ཏིང་ངེ་འཛིན་ཆུང་བའི་ཕྱིར་རོ། དེ་བཞིན་གཤེགས་པས་ནི་ཐམས་ཅད་གཟིགས་ཏེ། ཞི་གནས་དང་ལྷག་མཐོང་མཚུངས་པར་ལྡན་པའི་ཕྱིར་རོ། ཞི་གནས་ཀྱི་སྟོབས་ཀྱིས་ནི་མར་མེ་རླུང་གིས་མ་བསྐྱོད་པ་བཞིན་དུ་རྣམ་རྟོག་པའི་རླུང་རྣམས་ཀྱིས་སེམས་གཡོ་བར་མི་འགྱུར་རོ། ལྷག་མཐོང་གིས་ནི་ལྟ་བ་ངན་པའི་དྲི་མ་མཐའ་དག་སྤངས་པས་གཞན་དག་གིས་མི་ཕྱེད་དོ། ཟླ་བ་སྒྲོན་མེའི་མདོ་ལས་ཇི་སྐད་དུ། ཞི་གནས་སྟོབས་ཀྱིས་གཡོ་བ་མེད་པར་འགྱུར། །ལྷག་མཐོང་གིས་ནི་རི་དང་འདྲ་བར་འགྱུར། ཞེས་གསུངས་པ་ལྟ་བུའོ། དེ་ལྟ་བས་ན་གཉིས་ཀ་ལ་རྣལ་འབྱོར་དུ་བྱས་པར་གནས་སོ།

དེ་ལ་ཐོག་མར་རེ་ཞིག་རྣལ་འབྱོར་པས་གང་གིས་བདེ་བར་མྱུར་དུ་ཞི་གནས་དང་ལྷག་མཐོང་འགྲུབ་པར་འགྱུར་བ་ཞི་གནས་དང་ལྷག་མཐོང་གི་ཚོགས་ལ་ཇེ་བསྟེན་པར་བྱའོ། དེ་ལ་ཞི་གནས་ཀྱི་ཚོགས་གང་ཞེ་ན། མཐུན་པའི་ཡུལ་ན་གནས་པ་དང་། འདོད་པ་ཆུང་བ་དང་། ཆོག་ཤེས་པ་དང་།

བྱ་བ་མང་པོ་ཡོངས་སུ་སྤངས་པ་དང་། ཚུལ་ཁྲིམས་རྣམ་པར་དག་པ་དང་། འདོད་པ་ལ་སོགས་པའི་རྣམ་པར་རྟོག་པ་ཡོངས་སུ་སྤངས་པའོ།

དེ་ལ་ཡོན་ཏན་ལྔ་དག་དང་ལྡན་པ་ནི་མཐུན་པའི་ཡུལ་ཡིན་པར་ཤེས་པར་བྱ་སྟེ། གོས་དང་ཟས་ལ་སོགས་པ་ཚེགས་མེད་པར་རྙེད་པའི་ཕྱིར་རྙེད་སླ་བ་དང་། སྐྱེ་བོ་མི་སྲུན་པ་དང་དགྲ་ལ་སོགས་པ་མི་གནས་པའི་ཕྱིར་གནས་བཟང་བ་དང་། ནད་མེད་པའི་ས་ཡིན་པས་ས་བཟང་བ་དང་། གྲོགས་ཚུལ་ཁྲིམས་དང་ལྡན་པ་ལྟ་བུ་མཚུངས་པ་ཡིན་པས་གྲོགས་བཟང་བ་དང་། ཉིན་མོ་སྐྱེ་བོ་མང་པོ་དག་གིས་མ་གང་བའི་ཕྱིར་དང་། མཚན་མོ་སྒྲ་ཆུང་བའི་ཕྱིར་ལེགས་པར་ལྡན་པའོ། འདོད་པ་ཆུང་བ་གང་ཞེ་ན། ཆོས་གོས་ལ་སོགས་པ་བཟང་པོའམ་མང་པོ་ལ་ལྷག་པར་ཆགས་པ་མེད་པའོ། ཆོག་ཤེས་པ་གང་ཞེ་ན། ཆོས་གོས་ལ་སོགས་པ་ངན་ངོན་ཙམ་རྙེད་པས་རྟག་ཏུ་ཆོག་ཤེས་པ་གང་ཡིན་པའོ། བྱ་བ་མང་པོ་ཡོངས་སུ་སྤང་པ་གང་ཞེ་ན། ཉོ་ཚོང་ལ་སོགས་པ་ལས་ངན་པ་ཡོངས་སུ་སྤང་བ་དང་། ཁྱིམ་པ་དང་རབ་ཏུ་བྱུང་བ་གང་དག་ཏ་ཅང་སྨོས་འདྲིན་བྱེད་པ་ཡོངས་སུ་སྤང་བ་དང་། སྨན་བྱེད་པ་སྐར་མ་རྩི་བ་ལ་སོགས་པ་ཡོངས་སུ་སྤངས་པ་གང་ཡིན་པའོ།

ཚུལ་ཁྲིམས་རྣམ་པར་དག་པ་གང་ཞེ་ན། སྡོམ་པ་གཉིས་ཀ་ལ་ཡང་རང་བཞིན་དང་བཅས་པའི་ཁ་ན་མ་ཐོ་བ་དང་བཅས་པའི་བསླབ་པའི་གཞི་མི་འདྲལ་བ་དང་། བག་མེད་པར་རལ་ན་ཡང་སྐྱེན་པ་སྐྱེན་པར་འགྱོད་པས་ཆོས་བཞིན་དུ་བྱེད་པ་དང་། ཉན་ཐོས་ཀྱི་སྡོམ་པ་ལ་ཕམ་པ་བཅོས་སུ་མི་

རུང་བར་གསུངས་པ་གང་ཡིན་པ་དེ་ལ་ཡང་འགྱོད་པ་དང་ལྡན་པ་དང་། ཕྱིས་མི་བྱ་བའི་སེམས་དང་ལྡན་པ་དང་། སེམས་གང་གིས་ལས་དེ་བྱས་པའི་སེམས་དེ་ལ་ངོ་བོ་ཉིད་མེད་པར་སོ་སོར་རྟོག་པའི་ཕྱིར་རམ། ཆོས་ཐམས་ཅད་ངོ་བོ་ཉིད་མེད་པར་གོམས་པའི་ཕྱིར་དེའི་ཚུལ་ཁྲིམས་རྣམ་པར་དག་པ་ཁོ་ན་ཡིན་པར་བརྗོད་པར་བྱའོ། དེ་ནི་འཕགས་པ་མ་སྐྱེས་དགྲའི་འགྱོད་པ་བསལ་བ་ལས་ཁོང་དུ་ཆུད་པར་རིག་པར་བྱའོ། དེ་བས་ན་དེ་འགྱོད་པ་མེད་པར་བྱས་ལ་སྒོམ་པ་ལ་མངོན་པར་བརྩོན་པར་བྱའོ།

འདོད་པ་རྣམས་ལ་ཡང་ཚེ་འདི་དང་ཚེ་ཕྱི་མ་ལ་ཉེས་དམིགས་རྣམ་པ་མང་པོར་འགྱུར་བར་ཡིད་ལ་བྱས་ལ་དེ་དག་ལ་རྣམ་པར་རྟོག་པ་སྤང་བར་བྱའོ། རྣམ་པ་གཅིག་ཏུ་ན་འཁོར་བ་པའི་དངོས་པོ་སྡུག་པའམ་མི་སྡུག་པ་ཡང་རུང་སྟེ། དེ་དག་ཐམས་ཅད་ནི་རྣམ་པར་འཇིག་པའི་ཆོས་ཅན་མི་བརྟན་པ་སྟེ། གདོན་མི་ཟ་བར་དེ་དག་ཐམས་ཅད་དང་བདག་རིང་པོར་མི་ཐོགས་པར་འབྲལ་བར་འགྱུར་ན། བདག་དེ་ལ་ཅི་ཞིག་ལྷག་པར་ཆགས་པ་ལ་སོགས་པར་འགྱུར་སྙམ་དུ་བསྒོམས་པས་རྣམ་པར་རྟོག་པ་ཐམས་ཅད་སྤང་བར་བྱའོ།

ལྷག་མཐོང་གི་ཚོགས་གང་ཞེ་ན། སྐྱེས་བུ་དམ་པ་ལ་བརྟེན་པ་དང་། མང་དུ་ཐོས་པ་ཡོངས་སུ་བཙལ་བ་དང་། ཚུལ་བཞིན་སེམས་དཔའོ། དེ་ལ་སྐྱེས་བུ་དམ་པ་ཇི་ལྟ་བུ་ལ་བརྟེན་པར་བྱ་ཞེ་ན། གང་མང་དུ་ཐོས་པ་དང་། ཚིག་གསལ་བ་དང་། སྙིང་རྗེ་དང་ལྡན་པ་དང་། སྐྱོ་བ་བཟོད་པའོ།

དེ་ལ་མང་དུ་ཐོས་པ་ཡོངས་སུ་བཙལ་བ་གང་ཞེ་ན། གང་བཅོམ་

ལྡན་འདས་ཀྱི་གསུང་རབ་ཡན་ལག་བཅུ་གཉིས་པོ་ངེས་པའི་དོན་དང་དྲང་བའི་དོན་ལ་གུས་པར་བྱས་ཤིང་ཤིན་ཏུ་ཉན་པ་སྟེ། འདི་ལྟར་འཕགས་པ་དགོངས་པ་ངེས་པར་འགྲེལ་བ་ལས། འཕགས་པའི་གཏམ་འདོད་པ་བཞིན་དུ་མ་ཐོས་པ་ནི་ལྷག་མཐོང་གི་གེགས་ཡིན་ནོ། ཞེས་བཀའ་སྩལ་ཏོ། དེ་ཉིད་ལས། ལྷག་མཐོང་ནི་ཐོས་པ་དང་བསམས་པ་ལས་བྱུང་བའི་ལྟ་བ་རྣམ་པར་དག་པའི་རྒྱུ་ལས་བྱུང་བ་ཡིན་ནོ། ཞེས་གསུངས་སོ། འཕགས་པ་སྲིད་མེད་ཀྱི་བུས་ཞུས་པ་ལས་ཀྱང་། ཐོས་པ་དང་ལྡན་པ་ནི་ཤེས་རབ་འབྱུང་བར་འགྱུར་རོ། ཤེས་རབ་དང་ལྡན་པ་ནི་ཉོན་མོངས་པ་རབ་ཏུ་ཞི་བར་འགྱུར་རོ། ཞེས་བཀའ་སྩལ་ཏོ།

ཚུལ་བཞིན་བསམ་པ་གང་ཞེ་ན། གང་ངེས་པའི་དོན་གྱི་མདོ་སྡེ་དང་དྲང་བའི་དོན་གྱི་མདོ་སྡེ་ལ་སོགས་པ་ལེགས་པར་གཏན་ལ་འབེབས་པ་སྟེ། དེ་ལྟར་བྱང་ཆུབ་སེམས་དཔའ་ཐེ་ཚོམ་མེད་ན་བསྒོམ་པ་ལ་གཅིག་ཏུ་ངེས་པར་འགྱུར་རོ། དེ་ལྟ་མ་ཡིན་ན་ཐེ་ཚོམ་གྱིས་འཕྱུང་མོ་ཉུག་པའི་ཐེག་པ་ལ་འདུག་པ་ནི་ལམ་ཁ་དབྲག་གི་མདོར་ཕྱིན་པའི་མི་ལྟར་གང་དུ་ཡང་གཅིག་ཏུ་ངེས་པར་མི་འགྱུར་རོ།

རྣལ་འབྱོར་པས་ནི་དུས་ཐམས་ཅད་དུ་ཉ་དང་ཤ་ལ་སོགས་པ་སྤང་ཞིང་མི་མཐུན་པ་མ་ཡིན་པ་དང་། ཟས་ཚོད་ཟིན་པར་བཟའ་བར་བྱའོ། དེ་ལྟར་བྱང་ཆུབ་སེམས་དཔའ་ཞི་གནས་དང་ལྷག་མཐོང་གི་ཚོགས་མཐའ་དག་བསགས་པ་དེས་བསྒོམ་པ་ལ་འཇུག་པར་བྱའོ།

དེ་ལ་རྣལ་འབྱོར་པས་སྒོམ་པའི་དུས་ན་ཐོག་མར་བྱ་བ་ཅི་ཡོད་པ་ཐམས་ཅད་ཡོངས་སུ་རྫོགས་པར་བྱས་ལ། བཤང་གཅི་བྱས་ནས་སྒྲའི་ཚེར་མ་མེད་པ་ཡིད་དུ་འོང་བའི་ཕྱོགས་སུ་བདག་གིས་སེམས་ཅན་ཐམས་ཅད་བྱང་ཆུབ་ཀྱི་སྙིང་པོ་ལ་དགོད་པར་བྱའོ་སྙམ་དུ་བསམ་ཞིང་། འགྲོ་བ་མཐའ་དག་མངོན་པར་གདོན་པའི་བསམ་པ་ཅན་གྱིས་སྙིང་རྗེ་ཆེན་པོ་མངོན་དུ་བྱས་ལ། ཕྱོགས་བཅུ་ན་བཞུགས་པའི་སངས་རྒྱས་དང་བྱང་ཆུབ་སེམས་དཔའ་ཐམས་ཅད་ལ་ཡན་ལག་ལྔས་ཕྱག་བྱས་ནས། སངས་རྒྱས་དང་བྱང་ཆུབ་སེམས་དཔའི་སྐུ་གཟུགས་རི་མོ་ལ་སོགས་པ་མདུན་དུ་བཞག་གམ་གཞན་དུ་ཡང་རུང་སྟེ། དེ་དག་ལ་ཅི་ནུས་ཀྱིས་མཆོད་པ་དང་བསྟོད་པ་བྱས་ལ་རང་གི་སྡིག་པ་བཤགས་ནས་འགྲོ་བ་མཐའ་དག་གི་བསོད་ནམས་ལ་རྗེས་སུ་ཡི་རང་བར་བྱས་ལ། སྟན་ཤིན་ཏུ་འཇམ་པོ་བདེ་བ་ལ་རྗེ་བཙུན་རྣམ་པར་སྣང་མཛད་ཀྱི་སྐྱིལ་མོ་ཀྲུང་ལྟ་བུའམ། སྐྱིལ་མོ་ཀྲུང་ཕྱེད་དུ་ཡང་རུང་སྟེ། མིག་ཧ་ཅང་ཡང་མི་དབྱེ། ཧ་ཅང་ཡང་མི་གཟུམ་པར་སྣའི་རྩེ་མོར་གཏད་ཅིང་། ལུས་ཧ་ཅང་ཡང་མི་སྒུ། ཧ་ཅང་ཡང་མི་དགྱེ་བར་དྲང་པོར་བསྲངས་ལ་དྲན་པ་ནང་དུ་བཞག་སྟེ་འདུག་པར་བྱའོ། དེ་ནས་ཕྲག་པ་མཉམ་པར་བཞག་ལ་མགོ་མི་དམའ་ཞིང་ཕྱོགས་གཅིག་ཏུ་མ་ཡོ་བར་བཞག་སྟེ། སྣ་ནས་ལྟེ་བའི་བར་དྲང་པོར་བཞག་གོ །སོ་དང་མཆུ་ཡང་ཐ་མལ་པར་བཞག་གོ །ལྕེ་ཡང་ཡ་སོའི་དྲུང་དུ་གཞར་རོ། དབུགས་ཕྱི་ནང་དུ་རྒྱུ་བ་ཡང་སྒྲ་ཅན་དང་། ཛམས་པ་ཅན་དང་། དབུགས་ཆོད་པ་ཅན་དུ་མི་བཏང་གི །ཅི་

ནས་ཀྱང་མི་ཆོར་བར་དལ་བུ་དལ་བུས་ལྷུན་གྱིས་གྲུབ་པའི་ཚུལ་གྱིས་དབུགས་ནང་དུ་རྔུབ་པ་དང་ཕྱིར་འབྱུང་བ་དེ་ལྟར་བྱའོ།

དེ་ལ་ཐོག་མར་རེ་ཞིག་ཞི་གནས་བསྒྲུབ་པར་བྱ་སྟེ། ཕྱི་རོལ་གྱི་ཡུལ་ལ་རྣམ་པར་གཡེང་བ་ཞི་ནས་ནང་དུ་དམིགས་པ་ལ་རྒྱུན་དུ་རང་གི་ངང་གིས་འཇུག་ལ། དགའ་བ་དང་ཤིན་ཏུ་སྦྱངས་པ་དང་ལྡན་པའི་སེམས་ཉིད་ལ་གནས་པ་ནི་ཞི་གནས་ཞེས་བྱའོ། ཞི་གནས་དེ་ཉིད་ལ་དམིགས་པའི་ཚེ་དེ་ཁོ་ན་ལ་རྣམ་པར་དཔྱོད་པ་གང་ཡིན་པ་དེ་ནི་ལྷག་མཐོང་ཡིན་ཏེ། འཕགས་པ་དཀོན་མཆོག་སྤྲིན་ལས་ཇི་སྐད་དུ། ཞི་གནས་ནི་སེམས་རྩེ་གཅིག་པ་ཉིད་དོ། ལྷག་མཐོང་ནི་ཡང་དག་པར་སོ་སོར་རྟོག་པའོ། ཞེས་གསུངས་པ་ལྟ་བུའོ།

འཕགས་པ་དགོངས་པ་ངེས་པར་འགྲེལ་པ་ལས་ཀྱང་། བཅོམ་ལྡན་འདས། ཇི་ལྟར་ཞི་གནས་ཡོངས་སུ་ཚོལ་བར་བགྱིད་པ་དང་། ལྷག་མཐོང་ལ་མཁས་པ་ལགས། བཀའ་སྩལ་པ། བྱམས་པ་ངས་ཆོས་གདགས་པ་རྣམ་པར་གཞག་པ་འདི་ལྟ་སྟེ། མདོའི་སྡེ་དང་། དབྱངས་ཀྱིས་བསྙད་པའི་སྡེ་དང་། ལུང་དུ་བསྟན་པའི་སྡེ་དང་། ཚིགས་སུ་བཅད་པའི་སྡེ་དང་། ཆེད་དུ་བརྗོད་པའི་སྡེ་དང་། གླེང་གཞིའི་སྡེ་དང་། རྟོགས་པ་བརྗོད་པའི་སྡེ་དང་། དེ་ལྟ་བུ་བྱུང་བའི་སྡེ་དང་། སྐྱེས་པ་རབས་ཀྱི་སྡེ་དང་། ཤིན་ཏུ་རྒྱས་པའི་སྡེ་དང་། རྨད་དུ་བྱུང་བའི་ཆོས་ཀྱི་སྡེ་དང་། གཏན་ལ་ཕབ་པར་བསྟན་པའི་སྡེ་གང་དག་བྱང་ཆུབ་སེམས་དཔའ་རྣམས་ལ་བཤད་པ་དེ་དག་བྱང་ཆུབ་སེམས་དཔས་ལེགས་པར་ཐོས། ལེགས་པར་གཟུང་། ཁ་ཏོན་བྱང་བར་

བྱས། ཡིད་ཀྱི་ལེགས་པར་བརྟགས། མཐོང་བས་ཤིན་ཏུ་རྟོགས་པར་བྱས་ནས་དེ་གཅིག་པུ་དབེན་པར་འདུག་སྟེ་ནང་དུ་ཡང་དག་བཞག་ནས་ཇི་ལྟར་ལེགས་པར་བསམས་པའི་ཆོས་དེ་དག་ཉིད་ཡིད་ལ་བྱེད་ཅིང་སེམས་གང་གིས་ཡིད་ལ་བྱེད་པའི་སེམས་དེ་ནང་དུ་རྒྱུན་ཆགས་སུ་ཡིད་ལ་བྱེད་པས་ཡིད་ལ་བྱེད་དོ། དེ་ལྟར་ཞུགས་ཤིང་དེ་ལ་ལན་མང་དུ་གནས་པ་དེ་ལ་ལུས་ཤིན་ཏུ་སྦྱངས་པ་དང་སེམས་ཤིན་ཏུ་སྦྱངས་པ་འབྱུང་བ་གང་ཡིན་པ་དེ་ནི་ཞི་གནས་ཞེས་བྱ་སྟེ། དེ་ལྟར་ན་བྱང་ཆུབ་སེམས་དཔའ་ཞི་གནས་ཡོངས་སུ་ཚོལ་བར་བྱེད་པ་ཡིན་ནོ། དེས་ལུས་ཤིན་ཏུ་སྦྱངས་པ་དང་། སེམས་ཤིན་ཏུ་སྦྱངས་པ་དེ་ཐོབ་ནས་དེ་ཉིད་ལ་གནས་ཏེ། སེམས་ཀྱི་རྣམ་པར་གཡེང་བ་སྤངས་ནས་ཇི་ལྟར་བསམས་པའི་ཆོས་དེ་དག་ཉིད་ནང་དུ་ཏིང་ངེ་འཛིན་གྱི་སྤྱོད་ཡུལ་གཟུགས་བརྙན་དུ་སོ་སོར་རྟོག་པ་བྱེད། མོས་པར་བྱེད་དོ། དེ་ལྟ་ཏིང་ངེ་འཛིན་གྱི་སྤྱོད་ཡུལ་གཟུགས་བརྙན་དེ་དག་ལ་ཤེས་བྱའི་དོན་དེ་རྣམ་པར་འབྱེད་པ་དང་། རབ་ཏུ་རྣམ་པར་འབྱེད་པ་དང་། ཡོངས་སུ་རྟོག་པ་དང་། ཡོངས་སུ་དཔྱོད་པ་དང་། བཟོད་པ་དང་། འདོད་པ་དང་། བྱེ་བྲག་འབྱེད་པ་དང་། ལྟ་བ་དང་། རྟོག་པ་གང་ཡིན་པ་དེ་ནི་ལྷག་མཐོང་ཞེས་བྱ་སྟེ། དེ་ལྟར་ན་བྱང་ཆུབ་སེམས་དཔའ་ལྷག་མཐོང་ལ་མཁས་པ་ཡིན་ནོ། ཞེས་གསུངས་སོ།

དེ་ལ་རྣལ་འབྱོར་པ་ཞི་གནས་མངོན་པར་བསྒྲུབ་པར་འདོད་པས་ཐོག་མར་རེ་ཞིག་མདོའི་སྡེ་དང་། དབྱངས་ཀྱིས་བསྙད་པའི་སྡེ་ལ་སོགས་པ་གསུང་

རབ་མཐའ་དག་ནི་དེ་བཞིན་ཉིད་ལ་གཞོལ་བ། དེ་བཞིན་ཉིད་ལ་བབ་པ།
དེ་བཞིན་ཉིད་ལ་འབབ་པའོ་ཞེས་ཐམས་ཅད་བསྡུས་ཏེ་དེ་ལ་སེམས་ཉེ་བར་
བཞག་པར་བྱའོ། རྣམ་པ་གཅིག་ཏུ་ན་རྣམ་པ་ཇི་ཙམ་གྱིས་ཆོས་ཐམས་ཅད་
བསྡུས་པར་གྱུར་པ་ཕུང་པོ་ལ་སོགས་པ་དེ་ལ་སེམས་ཉེ་བར་བཞག་པར་བྱའོ།
རྣམ་པ་གཅིག་ཏུ་ན་ཇི་ལྟར་མཐོང་བ་དང་། ཇི་ལྟར་ཐོས་པའི་སངས་རྒྱས་
ཀྱི་སྐུ་གཟུགས་ལ་སེམས་གཞག་པར་བྱ་སྟེ། འཕགས་པ་ཏིང་ངེ་འཛིན་གྱི་
རྒྱལ་པོ་ལས་ཇི་སྐད་དུ།

གསེར་གྱི་ཁ་དོག་ལྟ་བུའི་སྐུ་ལུས་ཀྱིས། །འཇིག་རྟེན་མགོན་པོ་ཀུན་
ཏུ་མཛེས་པ་སྟེ། །དམིགས་པ་དེ་ལ་གང་གིས་སེམས་འཇུག་པ། །བྱང་
ཆུབ་སེམས་དཔའ་དེ་མཉམ་བཞག་ཅེས་བྱ། ཞེས་གསུངས་པ་ལྟ་བུའོ།

དེ་ལྟར་གང་ལ་འདོད་པའི་དམིགས་པ་དེ་ལ་སེམས་བཞག་ནས་དེ་
ཉིད་ལ་ཕྱིར་ཞིང་རྒྱུན་དུ་སེམས་བཞག་པར་བྱའོ། དེ་ལ་ཉེ་བར་བཞག་ནས་
སེམས་ལ་འདི་ལྟར་དཔྱད་པར་བྱ་སྟེ། ཅི་དམིགས་པ་ལེགས་པར་འཛིན་
ཏམ། འོན་ཏེ་བྱིང་ངམ། འོན་ཏེ་ཕྱི་རོལ་གྱི་ཡུལ་ལ་རྣམ་པར་འཕྲོར་བས་
རྣམ་པར་གཡེངས་སམ་སྙམ་དུ་བརྟག་པར་བྱའོ། དེ་ལ་གལ་ཏེ་རྨུགས་པ་
དང་གཉིད་ཀྱིས་ནོན་ནས་སེམས་བྱིང་ངམ། བྱིང་དུ་དོགས་པ་མཐོང་བ་
དེའི་ཚེ། མཆོག་ཏུ་དགའ་བའི་དངོས་པོ་སངས་རྒྱས་ཀྱི་སྐུ་གཟུགས་ལ་སོགས་
པའམ། སྣང་བའི་འདུ་ཤེས་ཡིད་ལ་བྱའོ། དེ་ནས་བྱིང་བ་ཞི་བར་བྱས་
ནས་ཅི་ནས་ཀྱང་དམིགས་པ་དེ་ཉིད་ལ་སེམས་ཀྱིས་དམིགས་པ་ཤིན་ཏུ་གསལ་

བར་མཐོང་བར་གྱུར་པ་དེ་ལྟར་བྱའོ།

གང་གི་ཚེ་དམུས་ལོང་ལྟ་བུའམ། མི་མུན་པར་ཞུགས་པ་ལྟ་བུའམ། མིག་བཙུམས་པ་ལྟ་བུར་སེམས་ཀྱིས་དམིགས་པ་ཤིན་ཏུ་གསལ་བར་མི་མཐོང་བ་དེའི་ཚེ་བྱིང་བར་གྱུར་བར་རིག་པར་བྱའོ། གང་གི་ཕྱི་རོལ་གྱི་གཟུགས་ལ་སོགས་པ་ལ་དེ་དག་གི་ཡོན་ཏན་རྟོག་པས་རྒྱུག་པའི་ཕྱིར་རམ། གཞན་ཡིད་ལ་བྱེད་པས་སམ། སྔོན་སྤྱོད་པའི་ཡུལ་ལ་འདོད་པས་སེམས་རྒོད་པའམ་རྒོད་དུ་དོགས་པར་མཐོང་བ་དེའི་ཚེ་འདུ་བྱེད་ཐམས་ཅད་མི་རྟག་པ་དང་། སྡུག་བསྔལ་བ་ལ་སོགས་པ་ཡིད་འབྱུང་བར་འགྱུར་བའི་དངོས་པོ་ཡིད་ལ་བྱའོ། དེ་ནས་རྣམ་པར་གཡེང་བ་ཞི་བར་བྱས་ནས་དྲན་པ་དང་ཤེས་བཞིན་གྱི་ཐག་པས་ཡིད་ཀྱི་གླང་པོ་ཆེ་དམིགས་པའི་སྡོང་པོ་དེ་ཉིད་ལ་གདགས་པར་བྱའོ། གང་གི་ཚེ་བྱིང་བ་དང་རྒོད་པ་མེད་པར་གྱུར་ཏེ། དམིགས་པ་དེ་ལ་སེམས་རྣལ་དུ་འཇུག་པར་མཐོང་བ་དེའི་ཚེ་ནི་རྩོལ་བ་གློད་ལ་བཏང་སྙོམས་སུ་བྱ་ཞིང་། དེའི་ཚེ་ཇི་སྲིད་འདོད་ཀྱི་བར་དུ་འདུག་པར་བྱའོ། དེ་ལྟར་ཞི་གནས་གོམས་པར་བྱས་པ་དེའི་ལུས་དང་སེམས་ཤིན་ཏུ་སྦྱངས་པར་གྱུར་པ་དང་། ཇི་ལྟར་འདོད་པ་བཞིན་དུ་དམིགས་པ་ལ་སེམས་རང་དབང་དུ་གྱུར་པ་དེའི་ཚེ་དེའི་ཞི་གནས་གྲུབ་པ་ཡིན་པར་རིག་པར་བྱའོ།

དེ་ནས་ཞི་གནས་གྲུབ་ནས་ལྷག་མཐོང་བསྒོམ་པར་བྱ་སྟེ། འདི་སྙམ་དུ་བསམ་པར་བྱའོ། བཅོམ་ལྡན་འདས་ཀྱི་བཀའ་ཐམས་ཅད་ནི་ལེགས་པར་གསུངས་པ་སྟེ། མངོན་སུམ་མམ་བརྒྱུད་པས་དེ་ཁོ་ན་མངོན་པར་གསལ་

བར་བྱེད་པ་དང་། དེ་ཁོ་ན་ལ་གཞོལ་བ་ཉིད་དོ། དེ་ཁོ་ན་ཤེས་ན་སྣང་བ་བྱུང་བས་མུན་པ་བསལ་བ་བཞིན་དུ་ལྟ་བའི་དྲ་བ་ཐམས་ཅད་དང་བྲལ་བར་འགྱུར་རོ། ཞི་གནས་ཙམ་གྱིས་ནི་ཡེ་ཤེས་དག་པར་མི་འགྱུར་ཞིང་སྒྲིབ་པའི་མུན་པ་ཡང་སེལ་བར་མི་འགྱུར་གྱི། ཤེས་རབ་ཀྱིས་ནི་དེ་ཁོ་ན་ལེགས་པར་བསྒོམས་ན་ཡེ་ཤེས་རྣམ་པར་དག་པར་འགྱུར། ཤེས་རབ་ཁོ་ནས་དེ་ཁོ་ན་ཉིད་རྟོགས་པར་འགྱུར། ཤེས་རབ་ཁོ་ནས་ཞི་གནས་སྒྲིབ་པ་ཡང་དག་པར་སྤོང་བར་འགྱུར་ཏེ། དེ་ལྟ་བས་ན་བདག་གིས་ཞི་གནས་ལ་གནས་ཏེ་ཤེས་རབ་ཀྱིས་དེ་ཁོ་ན་ཡོངས་སུ་བཙལ་བར་བྱའི། ཞི་གནས་ཙམ་གྱིས་ནི་ཆོག་པར་འཛིན་པར་མི་བྱའོ་སྙམ་དུ་བསམ་མོ།

དེ་ཁོ་ན་ཇི་ལྟ་བུ་ཞེ་ན། གང་དོན་དམ་པར་དངོས་པོ་ཐམས་ཅད་གང་ཟག་དང་ཆོས་ཀྱི་བདག་གཉིས་ཀྱིས་སྟོང་པར་ཉིད་དེ། དེ་ཡང་ཤེས་རབ་ཀྱི་ཕ་རོལ་ཏུ་ཕྱིན་པས་རྟོགས་པར་འགྱུར་གྱི། གཞན་གྱིས་ནི་མ་ཡིན་ཏེ། འཕགས་པ་དགོངས་པ་ངེས་པར་འགྲེལ་པ་ལས། བཅོམ་ལྡན་འདས་བྱང་ཆུབ་སེམས་དཔས་ཆོས་རྣམས་ཀྱི་ངོ་བོ་ཉིད་མ་མཆིས་པ་ཉིད་ཕ་རོལ་ཏུ་ཕྱིན་པ་གང་གིས་འཛིན་པ་ལགས། སྤྱན་རས་གཟིགས་དབང་ཕྱུག་ཤེས་རབ་ཀྱི་ཕ་རོལ་ཏུ་ཕྱིན་པས་འཛིན་ཏོ། ཞེས་ཇི་སྐད་གསུངས་པ་ལྟ་བུའོ། དེ་ལྟ་བས་ན་ཞི་གནས་ལ་གནས་ཏེ་ཤེས་རབ་བསྒོམ་པར་བྱའོ།

དེ་ལ་རྣལ་འབྱོར་པས་འདི་ལྟར་རྣམ་པར་དཔྱད་པར་བྱ་སྟེ། གང་ཟག་ནི་ཕུང་པོ་དང་ཁམས་དང་སྐྱེ་མཆེད་ལས་གུད་ན་མི་དམིགས་སོ། གང་

ཟག་ནི་ཕུང་པོ་ལ་སོགས་པའི་ངོ་བོ་ཉིད་ཀྱང་མ་ཡིན་ཏེ། ཕུང་པོ་ལ་སོགས་པ་དེ་དག་ནི་མི་རྟག་པ་དང་དུ་མའི་ངོ་བོ་ཡིན་པའི་ཕྱིར་དང་། གང་ཟག་ནི་རྟག་པ་དང་། གཅིག་པུའི་ངོ་བོ་ཡིན་པར་གཞན་དག་གིས་བརྟགས་པའི་ཕྱིར་རོ། དེ་ཉིད་དམ། གཞན་དུ་བརྗོད་དུ་མི་རུང་བའི་གང་ཟག་གི་དངོས་པོ་ཡོད་པར་མི་རུང་སྟེ། དངོས་པོ་ཡོད་པའི་རྣམ་པ་གཞན་མེད་པའི་ཕྱིར་རོ། དེ་ལྟ་བས་ན་འདི་ལྟ་སྟེ། འཇིག་རྟེན་གྱི་ང་དང་ངའི་ཞེས་བྱ་བ་འདི་ནི་འཁྲུལ་པ་ཁོ་ནའོ་ཞེས་དཔྱད་པར་བྱའོ།

ཆོས་ལ་བདག་མེད་པ་ཡང་འདི་ལྟར་བསྒོམས་པར་བྱ་སྟེ། ཆོས་ཞེས་བྱ་བ་ནི་མདོར་བསྡུས་ན་ཕུང་པོ་ལྔ་དང་། སྐྱེ་མཆེད་བཅུ་གཉིས་དང་། ཁམས་བཅོ་བརྒྱད་དོ། དེ་ལ་ཕུང་པོ་དང་། སྐྱེ་མཆེད་དང་། ཁམས་གཟུགས་ཅན་གང་དག་ཡིན་པ་དེ་དག་ནི་དོན་དམ་པར་ན། སེམས་ཀྱི་རྣམ་པ་ལས་གུད་ན་མེད་དེ། དེ་དག་རྡུལ་ཕྲ་རབ་ཏུ་བཤིག་ལ་རྡུལ་ཕྲ་རབ་རྣམས་ཀྱང་ཆ་ཤས་ཀྱི་ངོ་བོ་ཉིད་སོ་སོར་བརྟགས་ན་ངོ་བོ་ཉིད་ངེས་པར་གཟུང་དུ་མེད་པའི་ཕྱིར་རོ། དེ་ལྟ་བས་ན་ཐོག་མ་མེད་པའི་དུས་ནས་གཟུགས་ལ་སོགས་པ་ཡང་དག་པ་མ་ཡིན་པ་ལ་མངོན་པར་ཞེན་པའི་དབང་གིས་རྨི་ལམ་ན་དམིགས་པའི་གཟུགས་ལ་སོགས་པ་སྣང་བ་བཞིན་དུ་བྱིས་པ་རྣམས་ལ་སེམས་ཉིད་གཟུགས་ལ་སོགས་པ་ཕྱི་རོལ་དུ་ཆད་པ་བཞིན་དུ་སྣང་གི་དོན་དམ་པར་ན་འདི་ལ་གཟུགས་ལ་སོགས་པ་ནི་སེམས་ཀྱི་རྣམ་པ་ལས་གུད་ན་མེད་དོ་ཞེས་དཔྱད་པར་བྱའོ། དེ་འདི་སྙམ་དུ་ཁམས་གསུམ་པོ་འདི་ནི་སེམས་ཙམ་མོ་

སྣམ་དུ་སེམས་ཤིང་། དེས་དེ་ལྟར་ཆོས་བརྟགས་པ་མཐའ་དག་ནི་སེམས་ཁོ་ན་ཡིན་པར་རྟོགས་ནས་དེ་ལ་སོ་སོར་བརྟགས་ན་ཆོས་ཐམས་ཅད་ཀྱི་ངོ་བོ་ཉིད་ལ་སོ་སོར་བརྟགས་པ་ཡིན་ནོ་ཞེས་སེམས་ཀྱི་ངོ་བོ་ཉིད་ལ་སོ་སོར་རྟོག་གོ། དེ་འདི་ལྟར་དཔྱོད་དོ།

དོན་དམ་པར་ན་སེམས་ཀྱང་བདེན་པར་མི་རུང་སྟེ། གང་གི་ཚེ་བརྫུན་པའི་ངོ་བོ་ཉིད་གཟུགས་ལ་སོགས་པའི་རྣམ་པ་འཛིན་པའི་སེམས་ཉིད་སྣ་ཚོགས་ཀྱི་རྣམ་པར་སྣང་བ་དེའི་ཚེ་དེ་བདེན་པ་ཉིད་དུ་ག་ལ་འགྱུར། ཇི་ལྟར་གཟུགས་ལ་སོགས་པ་བརྫུན་པ་དེ་བཞིན་དུ་སེམས་ཀྱང་དེ་ལས་གུད་ན་མེད་པས་བརྫུན་པ་ཉིད་དོ། ཇི་ལྟར་གཟུགས་ལ་སོགས་པ་སྣ་ཚོགས་ཀྱི་རྣམ་པ་ཡིན་པས་གཅིག་དང་དུ་མའི་ངོ་བོ་ཉིད་མ་ཡིན་པ་དེ་བཞིན་དུ་སེམས་ཀྱང་དེ་ལས་གུད་ན་མེད་པའི་ཕྱིར་གཅིག་དང་དུ་མའི་ངོ་བོ་ཉིད་མ་ཡིན་ནོ། དེ་ལྟ་བས་ན་སེམས་ནི་སྒྱུ་མ་ལ་སོགས་པའི་ངོ་བོ་ཉིད་ལྟ་བུ་ཁོ་ནའོ།

སེམས་ཇི་ལྟ་བ་དེ་བཞིན་དུ་ཆོས་ཐམས་ཅད་ཀྱང་སྒྱུ་མ་ལ་སོགས་པའི་ངོ་བོ་ཉིད་ལྟ་བུ་ཁོ་ནའོ་ཞེས་དཔྱོད་དོ། དེས་དེ་ལྟར་ཤེས་རབ་ཀྱིས་སེམས་ཀྱི་ངོ་བོ་ཉིད་ལ་སོ་སོར་བརྟགས་ན་དོན་དམ་པར་སེམས་ནི་ནང་དུ་ཡང་མི་དམིགས། ཕྱི་རོལ་དུ་ཡང་མི་དམིགས། གཉིས་ཀ་མེད་པར་ཡང་མི་དམིགས། འདས་པའི་སེམས་ཀྱང་མི་དམིགས། མ་འོངས་པ་ཡང་མི་དམིགས། ད་ལྟར་བྱུང་བ་ཡང་མི་དམིགས་སོ། སེམས་སྐྱེ་བའི་ཚེ་གང་ནས་ཀྱང་མི་འོང་། འགག་པའི་ཚེ་གང་དུ་ཡང་མི་འགྲོ་སྟེ། སེམས་ནི་གཟུང་དུ་མེད་པ། བསྟན་

དུ་མེད་ཅིང་གཟུང་དུ་མེད་ལ་གཟུགས་ཅན་མ་ཡིན་པ་གང་ཡིན་པ་དེའི་ངོ་བོ་ཉིད་ཅི་འདྲ་ཞེ་ན། འཕགས་པ་དཀོན་མཆོག་བརྩེགས་པ་ལས་ཇི་སྐད་གསུངས་པ་ལྟ་བུ་སྟེ། འོད་སྲུངས་སེམས་ནི་ཡོངས་སུ་བཙལ་ན་མི་རྙེད་དོ། གང་མ་རྙེད་པ་དེ་མི་དམིགས་སོ། གང་མི་དམིགས་པ་དེ་འདས་པ་ཡང་མ་ཡིན། མ་འོངས་པ་ཡང་མ་ཡིན། ད་ལྟར་བྱུང་བ་ཡང་མ་ཡིན་ནོ། ཞེས་རྒྱ་ཆེར་འབྱུང་ངོ་། དེས་དེ་ལྟར་བཏགས་ན་སེམས་ཀྱི་དང་པོ་ཡང་དག་པར་རྗེས་སུ་མི་མཐོང་། ཐ་མ་ཡང་དག་པར་རྗེས་སུ་མི་མཐོང་། བར་མ་ཡང་དག་པར་རྗེས་སུ་མི་མཐོང་ངོ་།

ཇི་ལྟར་སེམས་ལ་མཐའ་དང་དབུས་མེད་པ་དེ་བཞིན་དུ་ཆོས་ཐམས་ཅད་ཀྱང་མཐའ་དང་དབུས་མེད་པར་ཁོང་དུ་ཆུད་དོ། དེས་དེ་ལྟར་སེམས་མཐའ་དང་དབུས་མེད་པར་ཁོང་དུ་ཆུད་ནས་སེམས་ཀྱི་ངོ་བོ་ཉིད་གང་ཡང་མི་དམིགས་སོ། སེམས་གང་གིས་ཡོངས་སུ་རྟོགས་པ་དེ་ཡང་སྟོང་པར་རྟོགས་སོ། དེ་རྟོགས་པས་སེམས་ཀྱི་རྣམ་པར་བསྒྲུབས་པའི་ངོ་བོ་ཉིད་གཟུགས་ལ་སོགས་པའི་ངོ་བོ་ཉིད་ཀྱང་ཡང་དག་པར་རྗེས་སུ་མི་མཐོང་ངོ་། དེས་དེ་ལྟར་ཤེས་རབ་ཀྱིས་ཆོས་ཐམས་ཅད་ཀྱི་ངོ་བོ་ཉིད་ཡང་དག་པར་རྗེས་སུ་མ་མཐོང་བས་གཟུགས་རྟག་གོ་ཞེའམ། མི་རྟག་གོ་ཞེའམ། སྟོང་ངོ་ཞེའམ། མི་སྟོང་ངོ་ཞེའམ། ཟག་པ་དང་བཅས་པའོ་ཞེའམ། ཟག་པ་མེད་པའོ་ཞེའམ། བྱུང་བའོ་ཞེའམ། མ་བྱུང་བའོ་ཞེའམ། ཡོད་པའོ་ཞེའམ། མེད་པའོ་ཞེས་རྟོག་པར་མི་བྱེད་དོ། ཇི་ལྟར་གཟུགས་ལ་རྟོག་པར་མི་བྱེད་པ་དེ་བཞིན་དུ་

ཚོར་བ་དང་། འདུ་ཤེས་དང་། འདུ་བྱེད་དང་། རྣམ་པར་ཤེས་པ་རྣམས་ལ་ཡང་རྟོག་པར་མི་བྱེད་དོ། ཆོས་ཅན་མ་གྲུབ་ན་དེའི་བྱེ་བྲག་རྣམས་ཀྱང་མི་འགྲུབ་པས་དེ་ལ་རྟོག་པར་ག་ལ་འགྱུར། དེས་དེ་ལྟར་ཤེས་རབ་ཀྱིས་རྣམ་པར་དཔྱད་དེ་གང་གི་ཚེ་རྣལ་འབྱོར་པས་དངོས་པོ་གང་གི་ངོ་བོ་ཉིད་དོན་དམ་པར་ངེས་པར་མི་འཛིན་པ་དེའི་ཚེ་རྣམ་པར་མི་རྟོག་པའི་ཏིང་ངེ་འཛིན་ལ་འཇུག་གོ །ཆོས་ཐམས་ཅད་ཀྱི་ངོ་བོ་ཉིད་མེད་པ་ཉིད་ཀྱང་རྟོགས་སོ།

གང་ཤེས་རབ་ཀྱིས་དངོས་པོའི་ངོ་བོ་ཉིད་སོ་སོར་བརྟགས་ནས་མི་བསྒོམ་གྱི། ཡིད་ལ་བྱེད་པ་ཡོངས་སུ་སྤོང་བ་ཙམ་འབའ་ཞིག་སྒོམ་པར་བྱེད་པ་དེའི་རྣམ་པར་རྟོག་པ་ནམ་ཡང་མི་ལྡོག་ཅིང་ངོ་བོ་ཉིད་མེད་པ་ཉིད་རྟོགས་པར་ཡང་མི་འགྱུར་ཏེ། ཤེས་རབ་ཀྱི་སྣང་བ་མེད་པའི་ཕྱིར་རོ། འདི་ལྟར་ཡང་དག་པར་སོ་སོར་རྟོག་པ་ཉིད་ལས་ཡང་དག་པ་ཇི་ལྟ་བ་བཞིན་དུ་ཤེས་པའི་མེ་བྱུང་ན་གཙུབ་ཤིང་གཙུབས་པའི་མེ་བཞིན་དུ་རྟོག་པའི་ཤིང་སྲེག་གོ །ཞེས་བཅོམ་ལྡན་འདས་ཀྱིས་བཀའ་སྩལ་ཏོ།

འཕགས་པ་དཀོན་མཆོག་སྤྲིན་ལས་ཀྱང་བཀའ་སྩལ་ཏེ། དེ་ལྟར་སྐྱོན་ལ་མཁས་པ་དེ་སྤྲོས་པ་ཐམས་ཅད་དང་བྲལ་བར་བྱ་བའི་ཕྱིར་སྟོང་པ་ཉིད་བསྒོམ་པ་ལ་རྣལ་འབྱོར་དུ་བྱེད་དོ། དེ་སྟོང་པ་ཉིད་ལ་བསྒོམ་པ་མང་བས་གནས་གང་དང་གང་དུ་སེམས་འཕྲོ་ཞིང་སེམས་མངོན་པར་དགའ་བའི་གནས་དེ་དང་དེ་དག་གི་ངོ་བོ་ཉིད་ཡོངས་སུ་བཙལ་ན་སྟོང་པར་རྟོགས་སོ། སེམས་གང་ཡིན་པ་དེ་ཡང་བརྟགས་ན་སྟོང་པར་རྟོགས་སོ། སེམས་གང་

གིས་རྟོགས་པ་དེ་ཡང་ངོ་བོ་ཉིད་ཀུན་ཏུ་བཙལ་ན་སྟོང་པར་རྟོགས་ཏེ། དེ་དེ་ལྟར་རྟོགས་པས་མཚན་མ་མེད་པའི་རྣལ་འབྱོར་ལ་འཇུག་གོ །ཞེས་འབྱུང་ངོ་། འདིས་ནི་ཡོངས་སུ་རྟོག་པ་སྔོན་དུ་གཏོང་བ་ཉིད་མཚན་མ་མེད་པ་ཉིད་ལ་འཇུག་པར་བསྟན་ཏོ།

ཡིད་ལ་བྱེད་པ་ཡོངས་སུ་སྤོང་བ་ཙམ་དང་། ཤེས་རབ་ཀྱི་དངོས་པོའི་ངོ་བོ་ཉིད་མི་དཔྱོད་པར་རྣམ་པར་མི་རྟོག་པ་ཉིད་དུ་འཇུག་པ་མི་སྲིད་པར་ཤིན་ཏུ་གསལ་བར་བསྟན་པ་ཡིན་ནོ། དེ་ལྟར་དེ་ཤེས་རབ་ཀྱིས་གཟུགས་ལ་སོགས་པའི་དངོས་པོའི་ངོ་བོ་ཉིད་ཡང་དག་པ་ཇི་ལྟ་བ་བཞིན་དུ་བརྟགས་ནས་བསམ་གཏན་བྱེད་ཀྱི། གཟུགས་ལ་སོགས་པ་ལ་གནས་ནས་བསམ་གཏན་མི་བྱེད་ཅིང་། འཇིག་རྟེན་འདི་དང་འཇིག་རྟེན་ཕ་རོལ་གྱི་བར་ལ་གནས་ནས་བསམ་གཏན་མི་བྱེད་དེ། གཟུགས་ལ་སོགས་པ་དེ་དག་མི་དམིགས་པའི་ཕྱིར་རོ། དེ་ལྟ་བས་ན་མི་གནས་པའི་བསམ་གཏན་པ་ཞེས་བྱའོ།

ཤེས་རབ་ཀྱིས་དངོས་པོ་མཐའ་དག་གི་ངོ་བོ་ཉིད་སོ་སོར་བརྟགས་ནས་གང་གི་ཕྱིར་མི་དམིགས་པར་བསམ་གཏན་བྱེད་པ་དེའི་ཕྱིར་ཤེས་རབ་མཆོག་གི་བསམ་གཏན་པ་ཞེས་བྱ་སྟེ། འཕགས་པ་ནམ་མཁའ་མཛོད་དང་། འཕགས་པ་གཙུག་ན་རིན་པོ་ཆེ་ལ་སོགས་པ་ལས་བསྟན་པ་བཞིན་ནོ།

དེ་ལྟར་གང་ཟག་དང་ཆོས་ལ་བདག་མེད་པའི་དེ་ཁོ་ན་ལ་ཞུགས་པ་དེ་ཡོངས་སུ་བརྟག་པར་བྱ་བ་བལྟ་བར་བྱ་བ་གཞན་མེད་པས་རྟོག་པ་དང་དཔྱོད་པ་དང་བྲལ་བ། བརྗོད་པ་མེད་པ་དང་གཅིག་ཏུ་གྱུར་པའི་ཡིད་ལ་

བྱེད་པ་རང་གི་ངང་གིས་འཇུག་པ་མངོན་པར་འདུ་བྱེད་པ་མེད་པས་དེ་ཁོ་ན་ཉིད་ལ་ཤིན་ཏུ་གསལ་བར་བསྒོམ་ཞིང་འདུག་པར་བྱའོ། དེར་གནས་ནས་སེམས་ཀྱི་རྒྱུན་རྣམ་པར་མི་གཡེང་བར་བྱའོ། གང་གི་ཚེ་བར་སྐབས་སུ་འདོད་ཆགས་ལ་སོགས་པས་སེམས་ཕྱི་རོལ་དུ་རྣམ་པར་གཡེང་བ་དེའི་ཚེ་རྣམ་པར་གཡེང་བ་ཚོར་བར་བྱས་ལ་མྱུར་དུ་མི་སྡུག་པ་བསྒོམ་པ་ལ་སོགས་པས་རྣམ་པར་གཡེང་བ་ཞི་བར་བྱས་ནས་མྱུར་དུ་དེ་བཞིན་ཉིད་ལ་སེམས་ཕྱིར་ཞིང་འཇུག་པར་བྱའོ། གང་གི་ཚེ་དེ་ལ་སེམས་མངོན་པར་མི་དགའ་བར་མཐོང་བ་དེའི་ཚེ་ཏིང་འཛིན་གྱི་ཡོན་ཏན་མཐོང་བས་དེ་ལ་མངོན་པར་དགའ་བ་བསྒོམ་པར་བྱའོ། རྣམ་པར་གཡེང་བ་ལ་ཉེས་པར་མཐོང་བས་ཀྱང་མི་དགའ་བ་རབ་ཏུ་ཞི་བར་བྱའོ། ཇི་སྟེ་རྨུགས་པ་དང་གཉིད་ཀྱིས་ནོན་ཏེ་རྒྱུ་བ་མི་གསལ་བས་སེམས་བྱིང་ངམ་བྱིང་དུ་དོགས་པར་མཐོང་བ་དེའི་ཚེ་གོང་མ་བཞིན་དུ་མཆོག་ཏུ་དགའ་བའི་དངོས་པོ་ཡིད་ལ་བྱེད་བ་ཞི་བར་བྱས་ལ། ཡང་དམིགས་པ་དེ་ཁོ་ན་དེ་ཉིད་ཤིན་ཏུ་དམ་པོར་གཟུང་བར་བྱའོ། ཇི་སྟེ་གང་གི་ཚེ་སྔོན་བགད་པ་དང་། རྩེས་པ་རྗེས་སུ་དྲན་པས་བར་སྐབས་སུ་སེམས་འཕྱུར་བའམ་རྒོད་དུ་དོགས་པར་མཐོང་བ་དེའི་ཚེ་གོང་མ་བཞིན་དུ་མི་རྟག་པ་ལ་སོགས་པ་ཡིད་འབྱུང་བར་འགྱུར་བའི་དངོས་པོ་ཡིད་ལ་བྱས་ལ་གཡེང་བ་ཞི་བར་བྱ་ཞིང་། དེ་ནས་ཡང་དེ་ཁོ་ན་ཉིད་ལ་སེམས་མངོན་པར་འདུ་བྱེད་པ་མེད་པར་འཇུག་པར་འབད་པར་བྱའོ།

ཇི་སྟེ་གང་གི་ཚེ་བྱིང་བ་དང་རྒོད་པ་དང་བྲལ་བར་གྱུར་ནས་མཉམ་

པར་ཞུགས་ཏེ་དེ་ཁོ་ན་ཉིད་ལ་སེམས་རང་གི་ངང་གིས་འཇུག་པར་འགྱུར་བ་དེའི་ཚེ་རྩོལ་བ་གློད་དེ་བཏང་སྙོམས་སུ་བྱའོ། གལ་ཏེ་སེམས་མཉམ་པར་ཞུགས་པ་ལ་བརྩལ་བ་བྱས་ན་དེའི་ཚེ་སེམས་རྣམ་པར་གཡེང་བར་འགྱུར་རོ། གལ་ཏེ་སེམས་བྱིང་བར་གྱུར་པ་ལ་བརྩལ་བར་མ་བྱས་ན་དེའི་ཚེ་ཤིན་ཏུ་བྱིང་བས་ལྷག་མཐོང་མེད་དེ། སེམས་དམུས་ལོང་གཞིན་དུ་འགྱུར་རོ། དེ་ལྟ་བས་ན་སེམས་བྱིང་བར་གྱུར་ན་བརྩལ་བར་བྱའོ། མཉམ་པར་གྱུར་ན་བརྩལ་བར་མི་བྱའོ། གང་གི་ཚེ་ལྷག་མཐོང་བསྒོམས་པས་ཤེས་རབ་ཤིན་ཏུ་ཤས་ཆེ་བར་གྱུར་པ་དེའི་ཚེ་ཞི་གནས་ཆུང་བས་མར་མེ་རླུང་ལ་བཞག་པ་བཞིན་དུ་སེམས་གཡོ་བར་འགྱུར་ཏེ། དེའི་ཕྱིར་དེ་ཁོ་ན་ཤིན་ཏུ་གསལ་བར་མཐོང་བར་མི་འགྱུར་ཏེ། དེ་བས་ན་དེའི་ཚེ་ཞི་གནས་བསྒོམ་པར་བྱའོ། ཞི་གནས་ཀྱི་ཤས་ཆེ་བར་གྱུར་ན་ཡང་ཤེས་རབ་བསྒོམ་པར་བྱའོ།

གང་གི་ཚེ་གཉིས་ཀ་མཉམ་དུ་འཇུག་པའི་ཚེ་ལུས་དང་སེམས་ལ་གནོད་པར་མ་གྱུར་གྱི་བར་དུ་མངོན་པར་འདུ་བྱེད་པ་མེད་པར་གནས་པར་བྱའོ། ལུས་ལ་སོགས་པ་ལ་གནོད་པར་གྱུར་ན་དེའི་བར་སྐབས་སུ་འཇིག་རྟེན་མཐའ་དག་སྒྱུ་མ་དང་། སྨིག་རྒྱུ་དང་། རྨི་ལམ་དང་། ཆུ་ཟླ་དང་། མིག་ཡོར་ལྟ་བུར་ལྟ་ཞིང་འདི་སྙམ་དུ་བསམ་པར་བྱ་སྟེ། སེམས་ཅན་འདི་དག་ནི་ཆོས་ཟབ་མོ་འདི་ལྟ་བུ་ཁོང་དུ་མ་ཆུད་པས་འཁོར་བ་ན་ཀུན་ཏུ་ཉོན་མོངས་པར་འགྱུར་གྱིས། བདག་གིས་ཅི་ནས་ཀྱང་དེ་དག་ཆོས་ཉིད་དེ་ཁོང་དུ་ཆུད་པར་འགྱུར་བ་དེ་ལྟར་བྱའོ་སྙམ་དུ་བསམ་ཞིང་། སྙིང་རྗེ་ཆེན་པོ་

དང་བྱང་ཆུབ་ཀྱི་སེམས་མངོན་དུ་བྱའོ། དེ་ནས་ངལ་བསོ་ལ། ཡང་དེ་
བཞིན་དུ་ཆོས་ཐམས་ཅད་སྣང་བ་མེད་པའི་ཏིང་ངེ་འཛིན་ལ་འཇུག་པར་བྱའོ།

ཡང་སེམས་ཤིན་ཏུ་སྐྱོ་བར་གྱུར་ན་དེ་བཞིན་དུ་ངལ་གསོ་བར་བྱའོ།
འདི་ནི་ཞི་གནས་དང་ལྷག་མཐོང་ཟུང་དུ་འབྲེལ་བར་འཇུག་པའི་ལམ་སྟེ་རྣམ་
པར་རྟོག་པ་དང་བཅས་པ་དང་། རྣམ་པར་མི་རྟོག་པའི་གཟུགས་བརྙན་ལ་
དམིགས་པའོ།

དེ་ལྟར་རྣལ་འབྱོར་པས་རིམ་པ་འདིས་ཆུ་ཚོད་གཅིག་གམ། མེལ་
ཚེ་ཐུན་ཕྱེད་དམ། ཐུན་གཅིག་གམ། ཇི་སྲིད་འདོད་ཀྱི་བར་དུ་དེ་ཁོ་ན་
བསྒོམ་ཞིང་འདུག་པར་བྱའོ། འདི་ནི་དོན་རབ་ཏུ་རྣམ་པར་འབྱེད་པའི་བསམ་
གཏན་ཏེ། འཕགས་པ་ལང་ཀར་གཤེགས་པ་ལས་བསྟན་ཏོ། དེ་ནས་འདོད་
ན་ཏིང་ངེ་འཛིན་ལས་ལངས་ཏེ་སྐྱིལ་མོ་ཀྲུང་མ་བཤིག་པར་འདི་སྙམ་དུ་ཆོས་
འདི་དག་ཐམས་ཅད་དོན་དམ་པར་ངོ་བོ་ཉིད་མེད་པ་ཉིད་ཡིན་དུ་ཟིན་ཀྱང་།
ཀུན་རྫོབ་ཏུ་རྣམ་པར་གནས་པ་ཉིད་དོ། དེ་ལྟ་མ་ཡིན་ན་ལས་དང་འབྲས་
བུ་འབྲེལ་བ་ལ་སོགས་པ་ཇི་ལྟར་རྣམ་པར་གནས་པར་འགྱུར། བཅོམ་ལྡན་
འདས་ཀྱིས་ཀྱང་། དངོས་པོ་སྐྱེ་བ་ཀུན་རྫོབ་ཏུ། །དམ་པའི་དོན་དུ་རང་
བཞིན་མེད། ཅེས་བཀའ་སྩལ་ཏོ།

སེམས་ཅན་བྱིས་པའི་བློ་ཅན་འདི་དག་ནི་ངོ་བོ་ཉིད་མེད་པའི་དངོས་
པོ་རྣམས་ལ་ཡོད་པ་ལ་སོགས་པ་སྒྲོ་འདོགས་པས་བློ་ཕྱིན་ཅི་ལོག་ཏུ་གྱུར་ཏེ།
ཡུན་རིང་པོར་འཁོར་བའི་འཁོར་ལོ་ན་ཡོངས་སུ་འཁྱམས་པས་བདག་གིས་

ཅི་ནས་ཀྱང་བསོད་ནམས་དང་ཡེ་ཤེས་ཀྱི་ཚོགས་བླ་ན་མེད་པ་ཡོངས་སུ་རྫོགས་པར་བྱ་སྟེ། དེ་ནས་ཐམས་ཅད་མཁྱེན་པའི་གོ་འཕང་ཐོབ་པར་བྱ་ལ། དེ་དག་ཆོས་ཉིད་ཁོང་དུ་ཆུད་པར་བྱའོ་སྙམ་དུ་བསམས་ལ།

དེ་ནས་དལ་བུས་སྐྱིལ་མོ་ཀྲུང་བཤིག་སྟེ་ཕྱོགས་བཅུ་ན་བཞུགས་པའི་སངས་རྒྱས་དང་བྱང་ཆུབ་སེམས་དཔའ་ཐམས་ཅད་ལ་ཕྱག་བྱས་ལ། དེ་དག་ལ་མཆོད་པ་དང་བསྟོད་པ་བྱས་ནས། འཕགས་པ་བཟང་པོ་སྤྱོད་པ་ལ་སོགས་པའི་སྨོན་ལམ་རྒྱ་ཆེན་པོ་གདབ་པོ། དེ་ནས་སྟོང་པ་ཉིད་དང་སྙིང་རྗེ་ཆེན་པོའི་སྙིང་པོ་ཅན་སྦྱིན་པ་ལ་སོགས་པ་བསོད་ནམས་དང་ཡེ་ཤེས་ཀྱི་ཚོགས་མཐའ་དག་བསྒྲུབ་པ་ལ་མངོན་པར་བརྩོན་པར་བྱའོ།

དེ་ལྟར་གྱུར་ན་བསམ་གཏན་དེ་རྣམ་པ་ཐམས་ཅད་ཀྱི་མཆོག་དང་ལྡན་པའི་སྟོང་པ་ཉིད་མངོན་པར་བསྒྲུབས་པ་ཡིན་ཏེ། འཕགས་པ་གཙུག་ན་རིན་པོ་ཆེ་ལས་ཇི་སྐད་དུ། དེ་བྱམས་པའི་གོ་ཆ་བགོས་ཤིང་སྙིང་རྗེ་ཆེན་པོའི་གནས་ལ་གནས་ནས་རྣམ་པ་ཐམས་ཅད་ཀྱི་མཆོག་དང་ལྡན་པའི་སྟོང་པ་ཉིད་མངོན་པར་བསྒྲུབ་པའི་བསམ་གཏན་བྱེད་དོ། དེ་ལ་རྣམ་པ་ཐམས་ཅད་ཀྱི་མཆོག་དང་ལྡན་པའི་སྟོང་པ་ཉིད་གང་ཞེ་ན། གང་སྦྱིན་པ་དང་མ་བྲལ་བ། ཚུལ་ཁྲིམས་དང་མ་བྲལ་བ། བཟོད་པ་དང་མ་བྲལ་བ། བརྩོན་འགྲུས་དང་མ་བྲལ་བ། བསམ་གཏན་དང་མ་བྲལ་བ། ཤེས་རབ་དང་མ་བྲལ་བ། ཐབས་དང་མ་བྲལ་བ། ཞེས་བྱ་བ་ལ་སོགས་པ་རྒྱ་ཆེར་བཀའ་སྩལ་པ་ལྟ་བུའོ། བྱང་ཆུབ་སེམས་དཔའ་ནི་སེམས་ཅན་ཐམས་ཅད་ཡོངས་

སུ་སྨིན་པར་བྱེད་པ་དང་། ཞིང་དང་། ལུས་དང་། གཡོག་འཁོར་མང་པོ་ལ་སོགས་པ་ཕུན་སུམ་ཚོགས་པར་འགྱུར་བའི་ཐབས་སྦྱིན་པ་ལ་སོགས་པའི་དགེ་བ་ངེས་པར་བསྟེན་པར་བྱ་དགོས་སོ།

དེ་ལྟ་མ་ཡིན་ན་སངས་རྒྱས་རྣམས་ཀྱི་ཞིང་ལ་སོགས་པ་ཕུན་སུམ་ཚོགས་པ་གང་བཀའ་སྩལ་པ་དེ་གང་གི་འབྲས་བུ་ཡིན་པར་འགྱུར། དེ་ལྟ་བས་ན་རྣམ་པ་ཐམས་ཅད་ཀྱི་མཆོག་དང་ལྡན་པ་ཐམས་ཅད་མཁྱེན་པའི་ཡེ་ཤེས་དེ་ནི་སྦྱིན་པ་ལ་སོགས་པ་ཐབས་ཀྱིས་ཡོངས་སུ་རྫོགས་པར་འགྱུར་བས་བཅོམ་ལྡན་འདས་ཀྱིས་ཐམས་ཅད་མཁྱེན་པའི་ཡེ་ཤེས་དེ་ནི་ཐབས་ཀྱིས་མཐར་ཕྱིན་པ་ཡིན་ནོ། ཞེས་བཀའ་སྩལ་ཏོ། དེའི་ཕྱིར་བྱང་ཆུབ་སེམས་དཔས་སྦྱིན་པ་ལ་སོགས་པ་ཐབས་ལ་ཡང་བསྟེན་པར་བྱའོ། སྟོང་པ་ཉིད་འབའ་ཞིག་ནི་མ་ཡིན་ནོ། དེ་སྐད་དུ་འཕགས་པ་ཆོས་ཐམས་ཅད་ཤིན་ཏུ་རྒྱས་པ་བསྡུས་པ་ལས་ཀྱང་བཀའ་སྩལ་ཏེ། བྱམས་པ་བྱང་ཆུབ་སེམས་དཔའ་རྣམས་ཀྱི་ཕ་རོལ་ཏུ་ཕྱིན་པ་དྲུག་ཡང་དག་པར་བསྒྲུབས་པ་འདི་ནི་རྫོགས་པའི་བྱང་ཆུབ་ཀྱི་ཕྱིར་ཡིན་ན། དེ་ལ་མི་བླུན་པོ་དེ་དག་འདི་སྐད་དུ། བྱང་ཆུབ་སེམས་དཔའ་ཤེས་རབ་ཀྱི་ཕ་རོལ་ཏུ་ཕྱིན་པ་ཁོ་ན་ལ་བསླབ་པར་བྱའི། ཕ་རོལ་ཏུ་ཕྱིན་པ་ལྷག་མ་རྣམས་ཀྱིས་ཅི་ཞིག་བྱ་ཞེས་ཟེར་ཞིང་། དེ་དག་ཕ་རོལ་ཏུ་ཕྱིན་པ་གཞན་དག་ལ་ཡང་སུན་འབྱིན་པར་སེམས་སོ། མ་ཕམ་པ་འདི་ཇི་སྙམ་དུ་སེམས། ཀཱ་ཤི་ཀའི་རྒྱལ་པོར་གྱུར་པ་གང་ཡིན་པ་དེས་ཕུག་རོན་གྱི་ཕྱིར་རང་གི་ཤ་ཁྲ་ལ་བྱིན་པ་དེ་ཤེས་རབ་འཆལ་བ་ཡིན་ནམ།

བྱམས་པས་གསོལ་བ། བཅོམ་ལྡན་འདས་དེ་ནི་མ་ལགས་སོ། བཅོམ་ལྡན་འདས་ཀྱིས་བཀའ་སྩལ་པ། བྱམས་པ་བྱང་ཆུབ་སེམས་དཔའི་སྤྱོད་པ་སྤྱོད་པ་ན་ཕ་རོལ་ཏུ་ཕྱིན་པ་དྲུག་དང་ལྡན་པའི་དགེ་བའི་རྩ་བ་གང་དག་བསགས་པའི་དགེ་བའི་རྩ་བ་དེ་དག་གིས་གནོད་པར་གྱུར་ཏམ། བྱམས་པས་གསོལ་བ། བཅོམ་ལྡན་འདས་དེ་ནི་མ་ལགས་སོ། བཅོམ་ལྡན་འདས་ཀྱིས་བཀའ་སྩལ་པ། མ་ཕམ་པ་ཁྱོད་ཀྱིས་ཀྱང་བསྐལ་པ་དྲུག་ཅུར་སྦྱིན་པའི་ཕ་རོལ་ཏུ་ཕྱིན་པ་ཡང་དག་པ་བསྒྲུབས། བསྐལ་པ་དྲུག་ཅུར་ཚུལ་ཁྲིམས་ཀྱི་ཕ་རོལ་ཏུ་ཕྱིན་པ། བསྐལ་པ་དྲུག་ཅུར་བཟོད་པའི་ཕ་རོལ་ཏུ་ཕྱིན་པ། བསྐལ་པ་དྲུག་ཅུར་བསམ་གཏན་གྱི་ཕ་རོལ་ཏུ་ཕྱིན་པ། བསྐལ་པ་དྲུག་ཅུར་ཤེས་རབ་ཀྱི་ཕ་རོལ་ཏུ་ཕྱིན་པ་ཡང་དག་པར་བསྒྲུབས་ན། དེ་ལ་མི་བླུན་པོ་དེ་དག་འདི་སྐད་དུ་ཚུལ་གཅིག་ཁོ་ནས་བྱང་ཆུབ་སྟེ། འདི་ལྟ་སྟེ། སྟོང་པ་ཉིད་ཀྱི་ཚུལ་གྱིས་སོ་ཞེས་ཟེར་ཏེ། དེ་དག་ནི་སྤྱོད་པ་ཡོངས་སུ་མ་དག་པར་འགྱུར་རོ། ཞེས་བྱ་བ་ལ་སོགས་པ་འབྱུང་ངོ་།

ཐབས་དང་བྲལ་ན་བྱང་ཆུབ་སེམས་དཔའི་ཤེས་རབ་འབའ་ཞིག་གིས་ནི་ཉན་ཐོས་བཞིན་དུ་སངས་རྒྱས་ཀྱི་མཛད་པ་བྱེད་མི་ནུས་ཀྱི། ཐབས་ཀྱིས་བསྡངས་ན་ནུས་པར་འགྱུར་ཏེ། འཕགས་པ་དཀོན་མཆོག་བརྩེགས་པ་ལས་ཇི་སྐད་དུ། འོད་སྲུང་འདི་ལྟ་སྟེ་དཔེར་ན་བློན་པོས་ཟིན་པའི་རྒྱལ་པོ་རྣམས་དགོས་པ་ཐམས་ཅད་བྱེད་པ་དེ་བཞིན་དུ་བྱང་ཆུབ་སེམས་དཔའི་ཤེས་རབ་ཐབས་མཁས་པས་ཡོངས་སུ་ཟིན་པ་དེ་ཡང་སངས་རྒྱས་ཀྱི་མཛད་པ་ཐམས་

ཅན་བྱེད་དོ། ཞེས་གསུངས་པ་ལྟ་བུའོ།

བྱང་ཆུབ་སེམས་དཔའ་རྣམས་ཀྱི་ལམ་གྱི་ལྟ་བ་ཡང་གཞན། མུ་སྟེགས་ཅན་དང་། ཉན་ཐོས་རྣམས་ཀྱི་ལམ་གྱི་ལྟ་བ་ཡང་གཞན་ཏེ། འདི་ལྟར་མུ་སྟེགས་ཅན་རྣམས་ཀྱི་ལམ་གྱི་ལྟ་བ་ནི་བདག་ལ་སོགས་པར་ཕྱིན་ཅི་ལོག་དང་ལྡན་པའི་ཕྱིར་ཐམས་ཅད་ཀྱི་ཐམས་ཅད་དུ་ཤེས་རབ་དང་བྲལ་བའི་ལམ་ཡིན་ཏེ། དེ་བས་ན་དེ་དག་ཐར་པ་མི་ཐོབ་བོ།

ཉན་ཐོས་རྣམས་ཀྱིས་ནི་སྙིང་རྗེ་ཆེན་པོ་དང་བྲལ་བས་ཐབས་དང་མི་ལྡན་པ་ཡིན་ཏེ། དེ་བས་ན་དེ་དག་གཅིག་ཏུ་མྱ་ངན་ལས་འདས་པ་ལ་གཞོལ་བར་འགྱུར་རོ། བྱང་ཆུབ་སེམས་དཔའ་རྣམས་ཀྱི་ལམ་ནི་ཤེས་རབ་དང་ཐབས་དང་ལྡན་པར་འདོད་དེ། དེ་བས་ན་དེ་དག་མི་གནས་པའི་མྱ་ངན་ལས་འདས་པ་ལ་གཞོལ་བར་འགྱུར་རོ། བྱང་ཆུབ་སེམས་དཔའ་རྣམས་ཀྱི་ལམ་ནི་ཤེས་རབ་དང་ཐབས་དང་ལྡན་པར་འདོད་དེ། དེས་ན་མི་གནས་པའི་མྱ་ངན་ལས་འདས་པ་ཐོབ་སྟེ། ཤེས་རབ་ཀྱི་སྟོབས་ཀྱིས་ནི་འཁོར་བར་མི་ལྟུང་ལ། ཐབས་ཀྱི་སྟོབས་ཀྱིས་ནི་མྱ་ངན་ལས་འདས་པར་མི་ལྟུང་བའི་ཕྱིར་རོ།

དེ་བས་ན་འཕགས་པ་ག་ཡཱ་མགོའི་རི་ལས། བྱང་ཆུབ་སེམས་དཔའ་རྣམས་ཀྱི་ལམ་ནི་མདོར་བསྡུ་ན་འདི་གཉིས་ཏེ། གཉིས་གང་ཞེ་ན། འདི་ལྟ་སྟེ། ཐབས་དང་ཤེས་རབ་བོ། ཞེས་བཀའ་སྩལ་ཏོ། འཕགས་པ་དཔལ་མཆོག་དང་པོ་ལས་ཀྱང་། ཤེས་རབ་ཀྱི་ཕ་རོལ་ཏུ་ཕྱིན་པ་ནི་མ་ཡིན་ནོ།

ཐབས་ལ་མཁས་པ་ནི་ཕ་ཡིན་ནོ། ཞེས་བཀའ་སྩལ་ཏོ།

འཕགས་པ་དྲི་མ་མེད་པར་གྲགས་པས་བསྟན་པ་ལས་ཀྱང་། བྱང་ཆུབ་སེམས་དཔའ་རྣམས་ཀྱི་འཆིང་བ་ནི་གང་། ཐར་པ་ནི་གང་ཞེ་ན། ཐབས་མེད་པར་སྲིད་པར་འགྲོ་བ་ཡོངས་སུ་འཛིན་པ་ནི་བྱང་ཆུབ་སེམས་དཔའི་འཆིང་བའོ། ཐབས་ཀྱིས་སྲིད་པའི་འགྲོ་བར་འགྲོ་བ་ནི་ཐར་པའོ། ཤེས་རབ་མེད་པར་སྲིད་པར་འགྲོ་བ་ཡོངས་སུ་འཛིན་པ་ནི་བྱང་ཆུབ་སེམས་དཔའི་འཆིང་བའོ། ཤེས་རབ་ཀྱིས་སྲིད་པའི་འགྲོ་བར་འགྲོ་བ་ནི་ཐར་པའོ། ཐབས་ཀྱིས་མ་ཟིན་པའི་ཤེས་རབ་ནི་འཆིང་བའོ། ཐབས་ཀྱིས་ཟིན་པའི་ཤེས་རབ་ནི་ཐར་པའོ། ཤེས་རབ་ཀྱིས་མ་ཟིན་པའི་ཐབས་ནི་འཆིང་བའོ། ཤེས་རབ་ཀྱིས་ཟིན་པའི་ཐབས་ནི་ཐར་པའོ། ཞེས་རྒྱ་ཆེར་བཀའ་སྩལ་ཏོ།

བྱང་ཆུབ་སེམས་དཔས་ཤེས་རབ་ཙམ་བསྟེན་ན་ནི་ཉན་ཐོས་ཀྱིས་འདོད་པའི་མྱ་ངན་ལས་འདས་པར་ལྷུང་བས་འཆིང་བ་བཞིན་དུ་འགྱུར་ཏེ། མི་གནས་པའི་མྱ་ངན་ལས་འདས་པས་གྲོལ་བར་མི་འགྱུར་རོ། དེ་ལྟ་བས་ན་ཐབས་དང་བྲལ་བའི་ཤེས་རབ་ནི་བྱང་ཆུབ་སེམས་དཔའ་རྣམས་ཀྱི་འཆིང་བའོ། ཞེས་བྱའོ། དེ་ལྟ་བས་ན་ལྷགས་པས་ཉེན་པ་ལ་མེ་བསྟེན་པ་བཞིན་དུ་བྱང་ཆུབ་སེམས་དཔས་ཕྱིན་ཅི་ལོག་གི་ལྷགས་པ་ཙམ་སྤང་བའི་ཕྱིར་ཐབས་དང་བཅས་པའི་ཤེས་རབ་ཀྱིས་སྟོང་པ་ཉིད་བསྟེན་པར་བྱའོ། ཉན་ཐོས་བཞིན་དུ་མངོན་དུ་ནི་མི་བྱ་སྟེ། འཕགས་པ་ཆོས་བཅུ་པའི་མདོ་ལས་ཇི་སྐད་དུ། རིགས་ཀྱི་བུ་འདི་ལྟ་སྟེ། དཔེར་ན་མི་ལ་ལ་ཞིག་མེ་ཡོངས་སུ་སྤྱོད་པར་གྱུར་

ཏེ། དེ་མི་དེ་ལ་བསྙི་སྐང་བྱེད། བླ་མར་བྱེད་ཀྱང་དེ་འདི་སྙམ་དུ་བདག་གིས་མི་དེ་བསྙི་སྐང་བྱས། བླ་མར་བྱས། རི་མོར་བྱས་ཀྱང་འདི་ལ་ལག་པ་གཉིས་ཀྱིས་ཡོངས་སུ་གཟུང་བར་བྱའོ་སྙམ་དུ་མི་སེམས་སོ། དེ་ཅིའི་ཕྱིར་ཞེ་ན། གཞི་དེ་ལས་བདག་ལ་ལུས་ཀྱི་སྡུག་བསྔལ་བའམ། སེམས་ཀྱི་ཡིད་མི་བདེ་བར་འགྱུར་དུ་འོང་སྙམ་པའི་ཕྱིར་རོ། དེ་བཞིན་དུ་བྱང་ཆུབ་སེམས་དཔའ་ཡང་མྱ་ངན་ལས་འདས་པའི་བསམ་པ་ཅན་ཡང་ཡིན་ལ་མྱ་ངན་ལས་འདས་པ་མངོན་སུམ་དུ་ཡང་མི་བྱེད་དོ། དེ་ཅིའི་ཕྱིར་ཞེ་ན། གཞི་དེ་ལས་བདག་བྱང་ཆུབ་ལས་ཕྱིར་ལྡོག་པར་འགྱུར་དུ་འོང་སྙམ་པའི་ཕྱིར་རོ། ཞེས་བཀའ་སྩལ་པ་ལྟ་བུའོ།

ཐབས་ཙམ་འབའ་ཞིག་བསྟེན་ན་ཡང་བྱང་ཆུབ་སེམས་དཔའ་སོ་སོའི་སྐྱེ་བའི་ས་ལས་མ་འདའ་བས་ཤིན་ཏུ་བཅིངས་པ་ཁོ་ན་འགྱུར་རོ། དེ་ལྟ་བས་ན་ཤེས་རབ་དང་བཅས་པའི་ཐབས་བསྟེན་པར་བྱ་སྟེ། འདི་ལྟར་སྔགས་ཀྱིས་ཡོངས་སུ་ཟིན་པའི་དུག་བཞིན་དུ་བྱང་ཆུབ་སེམས་དཔའ་རྣམས་ཀྱི་ཉོན་མོངས་པ་ཡང་ཤེས་རབ་ཀྱིས་ཡོངས་སུ་ཟིན་པའི་སྟོབས་ཀྱིས་བསྒོམས་ན་བདུད་རྩིར་འགྱུར་ན། རང་བཞིན་གྱིས་མངོན་པར་མཐོ་བའི་འབྲས་བུ་ཅན་སྦྱིན་པ་ལ་སོགས་པ་གང་ཡིན་པ་ལྟ་སྨོས་ཀྱང་ཅི་དགོས་ཏེ། འཕགས་པ་དཀོན་མཆོག་བརྩེགས་པ་ལས་ཇི་སྐད་དུ། འོད་སྲུངས་འདི་ལྟ་སྟེ། དཔེར་ན་སྔགས་དང་སྨན་གྱིས་ཡོངས་སུ་ཟིན་པའི་དུག་གིས་ནི་འཆི་བར་བྱེད་མི་ནུས་སོ། དེ་བཞིན་དུ་བྱང་ཆུབ་སེམས་དཔའ་རྣམས་ཀྱི་ཉོན་མོངས་པ་ཤེས་

རབ་ཀྱིས་ཡོངས་སུ་ཟིན་པས་ཀྱང་ལོག་པར་ལྟུང་བར་བྱེད་མི་ནུས་སོ། ཞེས་བཀའ་སྩལ་ཏོ།

དེ་ལྟ་བས་ན་གང་གི་ཕྱིར་བྱང་ཆུབ་སེམས་དཔའ་ཐབས་ཀྱི་སྟོབས་ཀྱིས་འཁོར་བ་མི་འདོར་བ་དེའི་ཕྱིར་མྱ་ངན་ལས་འདས་པར་མི་ལྟུང་ངོ་། གང་གི་ཕྱིར་ཤེས་རབ་ཀྱི་སྟོབས་ཀྱིས་དམིགས་པ་མཐའ་དག་སྤོང་བ་དེའི་ཕྱིར་འཁོར་བར་མི་ལྟུང་སྟེ། དེ་བས་ན་མི་གནས་པའི་མྱ་ངན་ལས་འདས་པ་སངས་རྒྱས་ཉིད་འཐོབ་བོ། དེ་བས་ན་འཕགས་པ་ནམ་མཁའ་མཛོད་ལས་ཀྱང་། དེ་ཤེས་རབ་ཀྱི་ཤེས་པས་ནི་ཉོན་མོངས་པ་ཐམས་ཅད་ཡོངས་སུ་འདོར་རོ། ཐབས་ཀྱི་ཤེས་པས་ནི་སེམས་ཅན་ཐམས་ཅད་ཡོངས་སུ་མི་གཏོང་ངོ་། ཞེས་བཀའ་སྩལ་ཏོ། འཕགས་པ་དགོངས་པ་ངེས་པར་འགྲེལ་པ་ལས་ཀྱང་། སེམས་ཅན་གྱི་དོན་ལ་ཤིན་ཏུ་མི་ཕྱོགས་པ་དང་། འདུ་བྱེད་མངོན་པར་འདུ་བྱ་བ་ཐམས་ཅད་ལ་ཤིན་ཏུ་མི་ཕྱོགས་པ་ནི་བླ་ན་མེད་པ་ཡང་དག་པར་རྫོགས་པའི་བྱང་ཆུབ་ཏུ་ངས་མ་བསྟན་ཏོ། ཞེས་བཀའ་སྩལ་ཏོ། དེ་ལྟ་བས་ན་སངས་རྒྱས་ཉིད་ཐོབ་པར་འདོད་པས་ཤེས་རབ་དང་ཐབས་གཉིས་ཀ་བསྟེན་པར་བྱའོ།

དེ་ལ་འཇིག་རྟེན་ལས་འདས་པའི་ཤེས་རབ་བསྒོམ་པའི་གནས་སྐབས་སམ། ཤིན་ཏུ་མཉམ་པར་གཞག་པའི་གནས་སྐབས་ན་སྦྱིན་པ་ལ་སོགས་པ་ཐབས་ལ་བསྟེན་པ་མི་འབྱུང་དུ་ཟིན་ཀྱང་། དེ་ལ་སྦྱོར་བ་དང་དེའི་རྗེས་ལས་བྱུང་བའི་ཤེས་རབ་གང་ཡང་བྱུང་བ་དེའི་ཚེ་ཐབས་ལ་བསྟེན་པ་འབྱུང་བ་ཉིད་དེ། དེའི་ཕྱིར་ཤེས་རབ་དང་ཐབས་གཉིས་ཅིག་ཅར་འཇུག་གོ། གཞན་

ཡང་བྱང་ཆུབ་སེམས་དཔའ་རྣམས་ཀྱི་ཤེས་རབ་དང་ཐབས་ཟུང་དུ་འབྲེལ་བར་འཇུག་པའི་ལམ་ནི་འདི་ཡིན་ཏེ། སེམས་ཅན་ཐམས་ཅད་ལ་ལྟ་བའི་སྙིང་རྗེ་ཆེན་པོས་ཡོངས་སུ་ཟིན་པས་འཇིག་རྟེན་ལས་འདས་པའི་ལམ་བསྟེན་པ་དང་། ལངས་པའི་ཐབས་ཀྱི་དུས་ན་ཡང་སྒྱུ་མ་མཁན་བཞིན་དུ་ཕྱིན་ཅི་མ་ལོག་པ་ཁོ་ནའི་སྦྱིན་པ་ལ་སོགས་པ་ལ་བསྟེན་པ་སྟེ། འཕགས་པ་བློ་གྲོས་མི་ཟད་པས་བསྟན་པ་ལས་ཇི་སྐད་དུ། དེ་ལ་བྱང་ཆུབ་སེམས་པའི་ཐབས་ནི་གང་། ཤེས་རབ་མངོན་པར་སྒྲུབ་པ་ནི་གང་ཞེ་ན། གང་གི་ཕྱིར་མཉམ་པར་བཞག་པ་ན་སེམས་ཅན་ལ་ལྟ་བས་ན་སྙིང་རྗེ་ཆེན་པོའི་དམིགས་པ་ལ་སེམས་ཉེ་བར་འཇོག་པ་དེ་ནི་དེའི་ཐབས་སོ། གང་གི་ཕྱིར་ཞི་བ་དང་རབ་ཏུ་ཞི་བར་སྙོམ་པར་འཇུག་པ་དེ་ནི་དེའི་ཤེས་རབ་བོ། ཞེས་རྒྱ་ཆེར་བཀའ་སྩལ་པ་ལྟ་བུའོ། བདུད་བཏུལ་བའི་ལེའུ་ལས་ཀྱང་བཀའ་སྩལ་ཏེ། གཞན་ཡང་བྱང་ཆུབ་སེམས་དཔའ་རྣམས་ཀྱི་སྦྱོར་བ་ཡང་དག་ཕུལ་ནི་ཤེས་རབ་ཀྱི་ཤེས་པས་མངོན་པར་བརྩོན་པར་ཡང་བྱེད་ལ། ཐབས་ཀྱི་ཤེས་པས་དགེ་བའི་ཆོས་ཐམས་ཅད་སྡུད་པར་ཡང་སྦྱོར་བ་དང་། ཤེས་རབ་ཀྱི་ཤེས་པས་བདག་མེད་པ་དང་། སེམས་ཅན་མེད་པ་དང་། སྲོག་མེད་པ་དང་། གསོ་བ་མེད་པ་དང་། གང་ཟག་མེད་པར་ཡང་སྦྱོར་ལ། ཐབས་ཀྱི་ཤེས་པས་སེམས་ཅན་ཐམས་ཅད་ཡོངས་སུ་སྨིན་པར་བྱེད་པ་ཡང་སྦྱོར་བ་གང་ཡིན་པའོ། ཞེས་རྒྱ་ཆེར་འབྱུང་ངོ་།

འཕགས་པ་ཆོས་ཐམས་ཅད་ཡང་དག་པར་བསྡུད་པའི་མདོ་ལས་

ཀྱང་། དཔེར་ན་སྒྱུ་མའི་མཁན་པོ་ཞིག །སྤྲུལ་པ་ཐར་བར་བྱ་ཕྱིར་བརྩོན། །དེས་ནི་སྔ་ནས་དེ་ཤེས་པས། །སྤྲུལ་པ་དེ་ལ་ཆགས་པ་མེད། །སྲིད་གསུམ་སྤྲུལ་པ་འདྲ་བར་ནི། །རྫོགས་པའི་བྱང་ཆུབ་མཁས་པས་ཤེས། །འགྲོ་བའི་ཆེད་དུ་གོ་བགོས་ཏེ། །འགྲོ་བ་དེ་ལྟར་སྔར་ནས་ཤེས། ཞེས་འབྱུང་ངོ་། བྱང་ཆུབ་སེམས་དཔའ་རྣམས་ཀྱི་ཤེས་རབ་དང་། ཐབས་ཀྱི་ཚུལ་ཁོ་ན་གྲུབ་པའི་དབང་དུ་མཛད་ནས། དེའི་སྦྱོར་བ་འཁོར་བ་ན་གནས་པ་ཡང་ཡིན་པ་ལ། བསམ་པ་མྱ་ངན་ལས་འདས་པ་ལ་གནས་པ་ཡང་ཡིན་ནོ། ཞེས་བཀའ་སྩལ་ཏོ།

དེ་ལྟར་སྟོང་པ་ཉིད་དང་སྙིང་རྗེ་ཆེན་པོའི་སྙིང་པོ་ཅན་བླ་ན་མེད་པ་ཡང་དག་པར་རྫོགས་པའི་བྱང་ཆུབ་ཏུ་ཡོངས་སུ་བསྔོས་པའི་སྦྱིན་པ་ལ་སོགས་པའི་ཐབས་གོམས་པར་བྱས་ལ། དོན་དམ་པའི་བྱང་ཆུབ་ཀྱི་སེམས་བསྐྱེད་པའི་ཕྱིར་སྔ་མ་བཞིན་དུ་རྟག་པར་དུས་དུས་སུ་ཞི་གནས་དང་ལྷག་མཐོང་གི་སྦྱོར་བ་ལ་ཅི་ནུས་སུ་བསྒོམ་པར་བྱ་སྟེ། འཕགས་པ་སྤྱོད་ཡུལ་ཡོངས་སུ་དག་པའི་མདོ་ལས། གནས་སྐབས་ཐམས་ཅད་དུ་སེམས་ཅན་གྱི་དོན་བྱེད་པའི་བྱང་ཆུབ་སེམས་དཔའ་རྣམས་ཀྱི་ཕན་ཡོན་ཇི་སྐད་དུ་བསྟན་པ་དེ་བཞིན་དུ་ཉེ་བར་གནས་པའི་དྲན་པས་དུས་ཐམས་ཅད་དུ་ཐབས་ལ་མཁས་པ་གོམས་པར་བྱའོ།

དེ་ལྟར་སྙིང་རྗེ་དང་། ཐབས་དང་། བྱང་ཆུབ་ཀྱི་སེམས་གོམས་པར་བྱས་པ་དེ་ཚེ་འདི་ལ་གདོན་མི་ཟ་བར་ཁྱད་པར་དུ་འགྱུར་ཏེ། དེས་

ནི་རྨི་ལམ་ན་རྟག་ཏུ་སངས་རྒྱས་དང་བྱང་ཆུབ་སེམས་དཔའ་མཐོང་བར་འགྱུར། རྨི་ལམ་བཟང་པོ་གཞན་དག་ཀྱང་རྨི་བར་འགྱུར། ལྷ་རྣམས་ཀྱང་ཡི་རངས་ནས་སྲུང་བ་བྱེད་པར་འགྱུར། སྐད་ཅིག་རེ་རེ་ལ་ཡང་བསོད་ནམས་དང་ཡེ་ཤེས་ཀྱི་ཚོགས་རྒྱ་ཆེན་པོ་སོགས་པར་འགྱུར། ཉོན་མོངས་པའི་སྒྲིབ་པ་དང་། གནས་ངན་ལེན་ཀྱང་སྦྱང་བར་འགྱུར། དུས་ཐམས་ཅད་དུ་ཡང་བདེ་བ་དང་ཡིད་བདེ་བ་མང་བར་འགྱུར། སྐྱེ་བོ་མང་པོ་ལ་སྡུག་པར་འགྱུར། ལུས་ལ་ཡང་ནད་ཀྱིས་མི་ཐེབས་པར་འགྱུར། སེམས་ལས་སུ་རུང་བ་ཉིད་ཀྱི་མཆོག་ཀྱང་ཐོབ་པར་འགྱུར་ཏེ། དེས་ན་མངོན་པར་ཤེས་པ་ལ་སོགས་པ་ཡོན་ཏན་ཁྱད་པར་ཅན་ཐོབ་བོ།

དེ་ནས་རྫུ་འཕྲུལ་གྱི་སྟོབས་ཀྱིས་འཇིག་རྟེན་གྱི་ཁམས་མཐའ་ཡས་པ་དག་ཏུ་སོང་ནས་སངས་རྒྱས་བཅོམ་ལྡན་འདས་རྣམས་ལ་མཆོད་པ་བྱེད་དོ། དེ་དག་ལ་ཆོས་ཀྱང་ཉན་ཏོ། འཆི་བའི་དུས་ཀྱི་ཚེ་ན་ཡང་གདོན་མི་ཟ་བར་སངས་རྒྱས་དང་བྱང་ཆུབ་སེམས་དཔའ་རྣམས་མཐོང་བར་འགྱུར་རོ། ཚེ་རབས་གཞན་ན་ཡང་སངས་རྒྱས་དང་བྱང་ཆུབ་སེམས་དཔའ་དང་མི་བྲལ་བའི་ཡུལ་དང་། ཁྱད་པར་དུ་འཕགས་པའི་ཁྱིམ་དུ་ཡང་སྐྱེ་བར་འགྱུར་ཏེ། དེས་ན་འབད་མི་དགོས་པར་བསོད་ནམས་དང་ཡེ་ཤེས་ཀྱི་ཚོགས་ཡོངས་སུ་རྫོགས་པར་བྱེད་དོ། ལོངས་སྤྱོད་ཆེ་བ་དང་། གཡོག་འཁོར་མང་བར་འགྱུར་རོ། ཤེས་རབ་རྣོ་བས་སྐྱེ་བོ་མང་པོ་ཡོངས་སུ་སྨིན་པར་ཡང་བྱེད་པར་འགྱུར་རོ། ཚེ་རབས་ཐམས་ཅད་དུ་ཚེ་རབས་དྲན་པར་འགྱུར་

ཏེ། དེ་ལྟར་ཕན་ཡོན་ཚད་མེད་པ་མདོ་གཞན་དག་ལས་འབྱུང་བ་ཁོང་དུ་ཆུད་པར་བྱའོ།

དེས་དེ་ལྟར་སྙིང་རྗེ་དང་། ཐབས་དང་། བྱང་ཆུབ་ཀྱི་སེམས་རྟག་ཏུ་གུས་པར་ཡུན་རིང་དུ་བསྒོམས་ན་རིམ་གྱིས་སེམས་ཀྱི་རྒྱུད་ཤིན་ཏུ་ཡོངས་སུ་དག་པའི་སྐད་ཅིག་འབྱུང་བས་ཡོངས་སུ་སྨིན་པར་འགྱུར་བའི་ཕྱིར་གཙུབ་ཤིང་གཙུབས་པའི་མེ་བཞིན་དུ་ཡང་དག་པའི་དོན་ལ་བསྒོམ་པ་རབ་ཀྱི་མཐར་ཕྱིན་པར་གྱུར་ནས་འཇིག་རྟེན་ལས་འདས་པའི་ཡེ་ཤེས་རྟོག་པའི་དྲ་བ་མཐའ་དག་དང་བྲལ་བ། ཆོས་ཀྱི་དབྱིངས་སྤྲོས་པ་མེད་པ་ཤིན་ཏུ་གསལ་བར་རྟོགས་པ། དྲི་མ་མེད་ཅིང་མི་གཡོ་ལ་མར་མེ་རླུང་མེད་པར་བཞག་པ་བཞིན་དུ་མི་གཡོ་བ་ཚད་མར་གྱུར་པ། ཆོས་ཐམས་ཅད་བདག་མེད་པའི་ངོ་བོ་དེ་ཁོ་ན་མངོན་དུ་བྱེད་པ་མཐོང་བའི་ལམ་གྱིས་བསྡུས་པ་དོན་དམ་པའི་བྱང་ཆུབ་ཀྱི་སེམས་ཀྱི་ངོ་བོ་ཉིད་འབྱུང་ངོ་། དེ་བྱུང་ནས་དངོས་པོའི་མཐའ་ལ་དམིགས་པ་ལ་ཞུགས་པ་ཡིན་ཏེ། དེ་བཞིན་གཤེགས་པའི་རིགས་སུ་སྐྱེས་པ་ཡིན། བྱང་ཆུབ་སེམས་དཔའི་སྐྱོན་མེད་པ་ལ་ཞུགས་པ་ཡིན། འཇིག་རྟེན་གྱི་འགྲོ་བ་ཐམས་ཅད་ལས་ལོག་པ་ཡིན། བྱང་ཆུབ་སེམས་དཔའི་ཆོས་ཉིད་དང་ཆོས་ཀྱི་དབྱིངས་རྟོགས་པ་ལ་གནས་པ་ཡིན། བྱང་ཆུབ་སེམས་དཔའི་ས་དང་པོ་ཐོབ་པ་ཡིན་ནོ་ཞེས་ཕན་ཡོན་དེ་རྒྱས་པར་ས་བཅུ་པ་ལ་སོགས་པ་ལས་ཁོང་དུ་ཆུད་པར་བྱའོ། འདི་ནི་དེ་བཞིན་ཉིད་ལ་དམིགས་པའི་བསམ་གཏན་ཏེ། འཕགས་པ་ལང་ཀར་གཤེགས་པ་ལས་བསྟན་ཏེ། འདི་ནི་བྱང་ཆུབ་སེམས

དཔའ་རྣམས་ཀྱི་སྤྲོས་པ་མེད་པ་རྣམ་པར་མི་རྟོག་པར་ཉིད་ལ་འཇུག་པའོ།

མོས་པས་སྤྱོད་པའི་ས་ལ་ནི་མོས་པའི་དབང་གིས་འཇུག་པར་རྣམ་པར་བཞག་གི །མངོན་པར་འདུ་བྱེད་པས་ནི་མ་ཡིན་ནོ། ཡེ་ཤེས་དེ་བྱུང་བར་གྱུར་ན་ནི་མངོན་དུ་ཞུགས་པ་ཡིན་ཏེ། དེ་ལྟར་ས་དང་པོར་ཞུགས་པ་དེ་ཕྱིས་བསྒོམ་པའི་ལམ་ལ་འཇིག་རྟེན་ལས་འདས་པ་དང་། དེའི་རྗེས་ལ་ཐོབ་པའི་ཡེ་ཤེས་གཉིས་ཀྱིས་ཤེས་རབ་དང་། ཐབས་བསྒོམས་པས་རིམ་གྱིས་བསྒོམ་པས་སྤང་བར་བྱ་བའི་སྒྲིབ་པ་བསགས་པ་ཕྲ་བ་བས་ཀྱང་ཆེས་ཕྲ་བ་སྦྱང་བའི་ཕྱིར་དང་། ཡོན་ཏན་ཁྱད་པར་ཅན་གོང་མ་གོང་མ་ཐོབ་པའི་ཕྱིར་ས་འོག་མ་རྣམས་ཡོངས་སུ་སྦྱོང་བས་དེ་བཞིན་གཤེགས་པའི་ཡེ་ཤེས་ཀྱི་བར་ལ་ཞུགས་ནས་ཐམས་ཅད་མཁྱེན་པ་ཉིད་ཀྱི་རྒྱ་མཚོར་འཇུག་ཅིང་དགོས་པ་ཡོངས་སུ་འགྲུབ་པའི་དམིགས་པ་ཡང་འཐོབ་སྟེ། འདི་ལྟར་རིམ་པ་ཁོ་ནར་སེམས་ཀྱི་རྒྱུད་ཡོངས་སུ་དག་པར་འཕགས་པ་ལང་ཀར་གཤེགས་པ་ལས་ཀྱང་བཀའ་སྩལ་ཏོ། འཕགས་པ་དགོངས་པ་ངེས་པར་འགྲེལ་པ་ལས་ཀྱང་། རིམ་གྱིས་ས་གོང་མ་གོང་མ་རྣམས་སུ་གསེར་ལྟ་བུར་སེམས་རྣམ་པར་སྦྱོང་ལ་བླ་ན་མེད་པ་ཡང་དག་པར་རྫོགས་པའི་བྱང་ཆུབ་ཀྱི་བར་དུ་མངོན་པར་རྫོགས་པར་འཚང་རྒྱའོ། ཞེས་གསུངས་སོ།

ཐམས་ཅད་མཁྱེན་པ་ཉིད་ཀྱི་རྒྱ་མཚོར་ཞུགས་པ་ན་ཡིད་བཞིན་གྱི་ནོར་བུ་ལྟ་བུར་སེམས་ཅན་མཐའ་དག་ཉེ་བར་འཚོ་བའི་ཡོན་ཏན་གྱི་ཕུང་པོ་དང་ནི་ལྡན། སྔོན་གྱི་སྨོན་ལམ་གྱི་འབྲས་བུ་ཡོད་པར་ནི་མཛད། ཐུགས་

ཧེ་ཆེན་པོའི་རང་བཞིན་དུ་ནི་འགྱུར། ལྷུན་གྱིས་གྲུབ་པའི་ཐབས་སྣ་ཚོགས་དག་དང་ལྡན། སྤྲུལ་པ་དཔག་ཏུ་མེད་པ་དག་གིས་འགྲོ་བ་མ་ལུས་པའི་དོན་དམ་རྣམ་པ་ཐམས་ཅད་ནི་མཛད། ཡོན་ཏན་ཕུན་སུམ་ཚོགས་པ་མ་ལུས་པ་རབ་ཀྱི་མཐར་ཕྱིན་པར་ནི་གྱུར། བག་ཆགས་དང་བཅས་པའི་ཉེས་པའི་དྲི་མ་མཐའ་དག་བསལ་ནས། སེམས་ཅན་གྱི་ཁམས་ཀྱི་མཐས་གཏུགས་པར་བཞུགས་པ་ཡིན་པར་རྟོགས་པ་དང་ལྡན་པས་སངས་རྒྱས་བཅོམ་ལྡན་འདས་ཡོན་ཏན་མཐའ་དག་གི་འབྱུང་གནས་ལ་དད་པ་བསྐྱེད་ལ་ཡོན་ཏན་དེ་ཡོངས་སུ་བསྒྲུབ་པའི་ཕྱིར་བདག་ཉིད་ཐམས་ཅད་ཀྱིས་འབད་པར་བྱའོ།

དེ་བས་ན་བཅོམ་ལྡན་འདས་ཀྱིས་འདི་སྐད་དུ། ཐམས་ཅད་མཁྱེན་པའི་ཡེ་ཤེས་དེ་ནི་སྙིང་རྗེའི་རྩ་བ་ལས་བྱུང་བ་ཡིན། བྱང་ཆུབ་སེམས་ཀྱི་རྒྱུ་ལས་བྱུང་བ་ཡིན། ཐབས་ཀྱིས་མཐར་ཕྱིན་པ་ཡིན་ནོ། ཞེས་བཀའ་སྩལ་ཏོ།

།དམ་པ་ཕྲག་དོག་ལ་སོགས་དྲི་མ་ཐག་བསྲིངས་པ།
།ཡོན་ཏན་རྣམས་ཀྱིས་མི་ངོམས་ཆུ་ཡི་མཚོ་འདྲ་དག
།རྣམ་པར་ཕྱེ་ནས་ལེགས་པར་བཤད་པ་རྣམས་འཛིན་བྱེད་དེ།
།ངང་པ་རབ་དགའ་ཆུ་ལས་འོ་མ་ལེན་པ་བཞིན།།

།དེ་ལྟ་བས་ན་མཁས་རྣམས་ཀྱིས།
།ཕྱོགས་ལྷུང་དཀྲུགས་ཡིད་རིང་སྤོངས་ལ།
།བྲིས་པ་ལས་ཀྱང་ལེགས་བཤད་པ།
།ཐམས་ཅད་བླང་བ་ཁོ་ནར་བྱ།།

།དེ་ལྟར་དབུ་མའི་ལམ་བཤད་པས།
།བདག་གིས་བསོད་ནམས་གང་ཐོབ་པ།
།དེ་ཡིས་སྐྱེ་བོ་མ་ལུས་པ།
།དབུ་མའི་ལམ་ནི་ཐོབ་པར་ཤོག།

བསྒོམ་པའི་རིམ་པ་ཨཱཙརྻཀམལཤཱིལས་བར་དུ་མཛད་པ་རྫོགས་སོ། རྒྱ་གར་གྱི་མཁན་པོ་པྲཛྙཱཝརྨ་དང་། ལོ་ཙཱ་བ་བནྡེ་ཡེ་ཤེས་སྡེས་བསྒྱུར་ཅིང་ཞུས་ཏེ་གཏན་ལ་ཕབ་པའོ།། །།